NAME DROPPING

NAME DROPPING

FRANK MILTON

E. P. Dutton New York

Lyrics on page vii from "Family Album" by Noël Coward are reprinted by permission of Chappell & Co., Ltd. Copyright © 1936 by Chappell & Co., Ltd. Copyright renewed. Published in the U.S.A. by Chappell & Co., Inc. International copyright secured. All rights reserved.

Lyrics on pages 115 and 116 from *All in Fun* are reprinted by kind permission of Blackwood Music Inc. & Fullness Music, Inc. Copyright © 1985 by Blackwood Music Inc. & Fullness Music, Inc. Administered by Blackwood Music Inc.

Published in the United States by E. P. Dutton,
a division of New American Library,
2 Park Avenue, New York, N.Y. 10016

Library of Congress Cataloging-in-Publication Data

Milton, Frank.
Name dropping.
1. Milton, Frank.—Friends and associates
—Anecdotes, facetiae, satire, etc. 2. Entertainers—
Anecdotes, facetiae, satire, etc. 3. Biography—20th
century—Anecdotes, facetiae, satire, etc. 4. Theatrical
producers and directors—United States—Biography.
5. Actors—United States—Biography. I. Title.
PN2287.M6435A36   1985   790.2'092'2 [B]   85-13045
ISBN 0-525-24368-2

Published simultaneously in Canada by
Fitzhenry & Whiteside Limited, Toronto

W

DESIGNED BY EARL TIDWELL

10 9 8 7 6 5 4 3 2 1

First Edition

Dedicated to the memory of Noël Coward

Here's a toast to each of us and all of us together—
Here's a toast to happiness and reasonable pride—
May our touch on life be lighter than a seabird's
    feather.
May all sorrows as we pass, politely step aside.

—NOËL COWARD, "Family Album"

PREFACE

I hope I know how to open and close. Having been an actor for twenty years, performing in shows such as *On the Town, Out of This World, Gentlemen Prefer Blondes, Tonight at 8:30,* and *Bells Are Ringing,* and in many flops and road tours and seasons of summer stock, I decided that I wasn't good-looking or tall enough to be Cary Grant, and certainly not talented enough to be Laurence Olivier. So I just stopped.

Some years later, I was in London and bought a few things for my apartment and somebody wanted to buy them from me for more than I had paid for them. At that moment I went into the antique business, commuting between London and New York and selling to all the decorators in New York. I loved every minute of it, crossing the Atlantic four or five times a year and coming into New York with forty pieces of luggage. I had a wonderful time, and miss it, but there is a moment to close every chapter, and when it came, I closed it.

One night about five years later, I ran into Hal Prince and he told me he was going to do a musical version of Ingmar Bergman's *Smiles of a Summer Night.* I thought that in his hands it was a brilliant idea and I raised some money for it, quite a bit in fact. I think that *A Little Night Music* was the perfect musical. By accident, I went to the first night of

Equus at the National Theatre in London and thought, "Whom do I kill to get my hands on this play?" Killing wasn't necessary, but I did manage to become the party of the third part as the associate producer. From there I went on to co-produce *Otherwise Engaged*, the London production of *A Little Night Music*, the New York production of Harold Pinter's *No Man's Land*, *Bedroom Farce*, and a resounding flop called *Harold and Maude*. I haven't stopped producing because of *Harold and Maude* (anybody can have a flop), but *Bedroom Farce* was supposed to be a hit, and it has been years and I have been able to pay off only part of the original backing. The theater is fine for actors and writers and dancers and singers and stagehands, etc., but after one gets finished paying all of them, there is too often nothing left for the independent producers or the backers. So I decided to stop that, too.

Before I start something else, I thought I'd catch up on what has happened—no easy task for someone who doesn't even like to send postcards, much less write a book! Mine has been a checkered career, but it's been filled with wonderful people, some of them monstrous but more often funny. I find name dropping irresistible—who doesn't?—mostly because the people behind the names have given me such pleasure and amusement through the years. I hope they give the reader some as well.

NAME DROPPING

ABBOTT, GEORGE

Mr. Abbott is now 98 years old. I ran into him about a year ago and said, "I had a dream about you last night. I dreamed that I auditioned for you and I *didn't* get the part." He said, *"Change* your dream."

I remember his coming to take over the direction of Cole Porter's *Out of This World* from Agnes de Mille. Cole Porter would sit and watch rehearsals, his malacca cane in hand, and his tie would get smaller every day and his boutonniere larger. Once he tried to make a suggestion to Mr. Abbott and Mr. Abbott said, "Later, Cole, later. I will take you to the Foltis Fisher Cafeteria for lunch." He then looked at the cast and said, "I want to teach Cole about the seamy side of life!"

Mr. Abbott is a brilliant craftsman. He would tell an actor to turn his head to the left, hit the last word in a sentence, and he would get a laugh—and did! He knew how to handle anybody—except Charlotte Greenwood. He told me that he had never been so nice to anybody, with such little result. He decided he would give her the full star treatment (which was a mistake). So he called the cast at 10:00 a.m. and Miss Greenwood at 11:00. She was incredible for her age, but she was old, and a Christian Scientist, and she arrived with a pet and wasn't about to change anything. He gave her a very friendly "Good morning," to which he got a grim reply, and said, "Let's take the tavern scene." Miss Greenwood had a line like "What are you all doing up here?" and Abbott suggested that it should be cut. She, again, grimly said, "It builds to the laugh." Abbott, still friendly, agreed to keep it in. A few lines later he wanted to cut another line, and Miss Greenwood, grimmer than ever, said, "It gets a laugh." Abbott said okay and gave up very quickly. He never called her again to rehearsal, and worked and rewrote the whole show around her. She refused to learn new lines. In the end the show was a flop. She came off better than anybody but ruined the evening.

In *Out of This World* I was very busy. I was the assistant stage manager. I played the bartender in the opening scene (for a hot five minutes I almost got to sing "From This Moment On"—the only song that was remembered from the show). I also was the understudy to William Redfield, who played Mercury. I begged Billy to stay off for a week but he wouldn't. One morning I got a call that I was going on that night, and I went to the theater early and started shaving. I didn't think that gods should have hair on their bodies. As I got the last hair off, Billy appeared in the doorway gasping for breath, and I wanted to take it from him. Anyway, I never got on. I also had to stand in the wings every night and watch Miss Greenwood sing "Nobody's Chasing Me," which was wonderful, finish her song, do her deep splits, and then back off into the wings, almost on her hands and knees, where I had to catch her. She was a very big lady.

Miss Greenwood would arrive at 4:00 p.m. and start stretching her legs at the bar so that at 11:00 p.m. that night she could do her split at the end of the show.

One day at the understudy rehearsal I was singing a terrible song called "Cherry Pies Ought to Be Me" (one of Cole's minor efforts), and she grabbed my hand and did it with me. When I finished, she said, "You will be wonderful and not to worry about understudying, but make sure that when you turn me at the end of the number my right profile shows and not my left, because I have a tooth missing in the back and I wouldn't want the audience to see it."

Early in rehearsals for *On the Town* I was just in the singing chorus and I thought, That will never do. I went to the conductor, Max Goberman, and said that if there were any lines leading to musical numbers to please keep me in mind. The opening line of the show is, "Have you got the time, Bud?" There is really nothing one can do except ask the question. Nevertheless, by the time we got to the first run-through of the opening for George Abbott, I must have sounded like Edmund Kean playing King Lear.

George Abbott smiled and said, "Don't give it a reading, Frank."

Three days later I found the part of the M.C., went to Abbott, and said I would like to read for it. He said "Okay. I will hear you at 4:15." At 4:15 I read for him and he said, "Perfect, never change it." I never did. For one year I kept singing "Happy Birthday." One night Mr. Abbott came to me and said, "You can't sing 'Happy Birthday' anymore—we have to change it to 'For He's a Jolly Good Fellow.' " I said I couldn't, that I was used to singing "Happy Birthday." But you can't say no to George Abbott. So when my big moment came, I bounced out on stage and sang, "For He's a Happy Birthday."

ADLER, STELLA

When Stella married Harold Clurman she told a friend that she was going to try it out in Brooklyn and if it worked she would bring it to New York.

An actor came up to her and said he would love to study with her but he didn't have the money. She said, "Steal it!"

Stella has had her face done—often. One day somebody ran into her and said, "What a great job

4

the last one was. You look better than ever." And Stella said, "It's a shame they can't lift my feet."

My first trip to Europe, thirty-five years ago, was the grand tour—London, Paris, Monte Carlo, Rome—and I ended up in Capri, which seemed paradise then, and it still does now. I went to a big dance the night before I was to sail back to America and found myself at midnight dancing with Stella in my arms. She asked me when I was going back home and I said that I was sailing the next day. She remembered her first trip to Europe. When she arrived back in New York it was hot. Her husband, Harold Clurman, met her at the boat at dinner time. Where can you go in America? They went to Dinty Moore's. It was noisy and full of sawdust. She didn't know what to order. Finally, she ordered a steak. It came—too thick. She picked up her knife and fork and was just about to start to eat when the waitress said, "Will you have your beverage with the main?" She said she put her knife and fork down, went home, and didn't leave her apartment for three weeks.

When Stella got to Florence after the war everybody kept saying, "David is coming back, David is coming back." They were talking about Michelangelo's David, but she thought they meant David Selznick.

Stella's first-term technique was brilliant. She was very careful to explain everything very, very slowly and clearly, dealing with the actors as though they were delicate musical instruments (she had studied with Stanislavski for years). She would always ask after she had finished explaining, "Do you understand, do you understand?" Everybody in class was terrified of her and one day she said, "Do you understand? Do you understand?" and one of the prettiest girls in class said, "I understand, Miss Adler"; Stella replied, "I don't care whether you understand," and went right to the young man next to her and said, "Do you understand?"

☆

Stella was in Sardi's one day having lunch with Sylvia Sydney when she saw Bennett Cerf (then publisher of Random House). She called him over to the table and said, "Bennett, I have just got home from three months in Europe. What books should I get to read? Oh, waiter, waiter, could I have a pencil and paper?" And she wrote down his suggestions. After she finished the list, she said, "Bennett, darling. Call me next week and we can have a meal, or something." While she was saying that, she was tearing up the list.

6

The entire Adler family have had their noses fixed. One day Stella was again having lunch with Sylvia Sydney, who was married to Luther Adler, Stella's brother. She said to Sylvia (who was pregnant), "You're a mess. You must fix yourself up. You will never get a job. Buy yourself a new dress and fix your hair and get a massage or something." And Sylvia replied, "I have to save for the baby's clothes and the baby's nurse and the baby's hospital bills." And Stella said, "Darling, start saving for the baby's nose job!"

Two young men were doing a scene from *Design for Living* and they were the last two who should have been doing it. Stella, if she were interested, would say, "Stay there"; if not, she would say, "Sit down." This time she said, "Sit down. You can't play Noël Coward unless you can say lightly 'I have cancer' every night." I told Noël this years later and he said, "That is exactly how to play my plays."

Stella's daughter got into trouble at school, so Stella was called with her daughter to the principal's office. They had to wait in the cafeteria. Stella, who had no conception of how to be a conventional mother, didn't know what to say to her daughter.

Finally she looked at her and said, "Eat something healthy."

☆

The definitive Stella story is the one she tells about her father, the great Yiddish actor Jacob Adler. He loved the ladies and one day he picked up a prostitute and took her back to his dressing room. In payment, he gave her two passes for the theater, and she said, "But Mr. Adler, I'm hungry," and he said, "I'm an actor, I give passes. You're hungry? Fuck a butcher."

AITKENS, THE

Maria (6'), Jonathan (6'3"), and Penelope (6')— when among the three of them, I always feel as though I am walking in a ravine. I love them all for different reasons. I feel as though I discovered Maria. I first saw her in a Tom Stoppard play that I hated. I asked her whether she could sing and she said no. I then asked her whether she could carry a tune and she said yes. I said, "Then you can sing." At a later date I was having a drink in New York with Hal Prince, because I was producing *A Little Night Music* in London, and he said he couldn't find anybody to play the Countess. I said, "I have the perfect person." Hal Prince thought I knew what I was doing, and she got the part. She was brilliant. Penelope (her mother,

8

Lady Aitken) I adore because she is always feeding me whenever I am in London. And Jonathan, her son, I adore because my shirts fit him and that makes me feel tall.

ALI, MUHAMMAD

I was walking down Sixth Avenue and I ran into Muhammad Ali and said, "You're the greatest," and he said, "You bet your ass I am."

ALLEN, RITA

I once told Rita that I should marry her to teach her how to spend her money—she just didn't know.

Years later she did marry. She and her husband bought a Rolls-Royce and a house in the country, and every weekend they would drive for about an hour and a half in the Rolls. By the time she got to the house, she would have terrible pains in her legs. The pains wouldn't go away until she drove to a restaurant and would then subside while she was having dinner and start again on the way back to New York. She finally found out that she was too short for the Rolls.

ALLERS, FRANZ

Franz Allers was the conductor of the original production of *My Fair Lady* and also of a musical play called *Happy as Larry*, starring Burgess Meredith. I was a featured player, and we had the first orchestra reading in an ice-cold theater in Boston. I had the opening song and Franz was in the orchestra pit. Sitting in the auditorium were Alexander Calder (who did the mobiles for the show) and a very avant-garde composer called Verez. We had been rehearsing for five weeks with just a piano. Suddenly Franz was giving me the intro to my number and it sounded like a fight between spoons, knives, and forks. When he cued me in, I didn't open my mouth. I said, "Franz, are you out of your mind? I must have a note." So Franz did the same intro, except this time an E flat was struck on the piano after all the clattering cutlery, and I started to sing.

ANDERSON, JUDITH

In 1947 I went to the opening of Judith Anderson in *Medea* and Noël Coward came up the aisle and said, "The trouble with that woman is that she got up on the wrong side of bed this morning!"

Once while she was playing *Medea*, declaiming to the audience, one of the girls in the Greek chorus kept making odd hissing noises at her. When she finally had a moment to turn around, she whispered to the girl, "What is it?" and the girl said, "You've got something on your face—right there," pointing to a large mole.

ANDREWS, DANA

He once told me that he had some rather effete friends who were driving through the Sahara when their car broke down and an enormous, very strong Arab rode down the hill. They quickly locked the doors and windows and the Arab kept pounding on the roof and started to shake the whole car. They timidly opened the window a crack and asked, "What do you want?" and the Arab said, "Do you know Cecil Beaton?"

ASTAIRE, ADELE

Adele was adorable and always hugged me when she saw me because she said I felt like her brother (one of the great compliments of my life).

AUER, MISCHA

A Russian friend of mine took me to Mischa's birthday party in about an eight-floor walk-up. It was black tie. On a blackboard was printed "Russian

Imperial Menu." It was a two-room, rather seedy apartment and there were twelve for dinner. Everybody was served straight vodka and somebody in the room stood up and said, "The Czar." I whispered to my Russian friend, "Do they think he is coming back?" and she nodded yes.

BALDWIN, BILLY

I had an antique shop in my flat in New York. One of my first customers was Billy Baldwin, who bought out my stock. He never asked a price, and flicking his ash into a very expensive piece of porcelain, inquired if it was an ashtray. When I said no, he replied, "It is now" and bought it. Oh, what style!

BANKHEAD, TALLULAH

The stories go on and on and on.

☆

When I moved into the Elysee, the whole hotel revolved around Tallulah. If I wanted to order dinner, the waiter would say, "Miss Bankhead had the lamb chops." One night, I saw Miss Bankhead in the lobby at 3:00 a.m. and she said, "Darling, do you play bridge?" I said, "Very badly." She said, "Be in my suite in fifteen minutes." I replied, "Miss

Bankhead, it's three o'clock in the morning." She asked me what I did in life and I told her I was an actor. She said I would never succeed. She was right, I should have played bridge.

There was a very ugly man in London years ago and, for the sake of the story, we will call him Lord Henry. Tallulah ran into a girl friend who asked her what she had done the night before and she said, "I went out with Lord Henry." The girl friend said, "Oh, my God, what did you do?" Tallulah replied, "I went down on him—anything, darling, anything to get away from that face!"

A friend went with Tallulah to a summer-stock production of a play starring Faye Emerson. The curtain rose and Faye made her entrance and read her first line. Tallulah, in a voice that carried to the mezzanine, exclaimed, "I can't understand a word she is saying." At the next line she started to cough. For the entire play she alternately coughed or said, "I can't understand a word she is saying." After the curtain came down, she turned to her friend and said that since everyone knew she was there, she should go backstage. She flew into Faye's dressing room declaring, "Darling, my friend couldn't understand a word you said."

There was a very fat, rich Texan, who has now left us, and who, while he was alive and boring everybody to death, was dying to meet Tallulah. When his big moment arrived and somebody introduced them, Tallulah took one look and said, "Unless you are very rich—there is no excuse for you."

Some years ago the director of *Regina*—the musical version of *The Little Foxes*, starring Jane Pickens—ran into Tallulah, who asked, "Who is playing my part?" He told her and she said, "What?" He repeated the name and she said, "In the first place she should change it, and in the second place I wouldn't be her if I were me."

BARRACCO, BARON

Stano is an old Roman friend and one of the worst snobs I have known (he is always talking about those upstarts in Buckingham Palace). One day in Rome while we were sitting on the Via Veneto, a stupid young Italian-American came over to our table and started talking Italian to Stano (who had been brought up with an English nanny and spoke English far better than I do). Stano was charming. However, when the young man left the table he said, "Even the cuff links were wrong."

BARRYMORE, ETHEL

I never met—as Metro Goldwyn Mayer used to say—Miss Ethel Barrymore, although we did live in the same flat at the Hotel Elysee at different times. However, there is certainly a story worth repeating about her.

She was directing in summer stock and there was an ingenue who was about to make her entrance when Miss Barrymore said, "Now, my child, come onstage, go up to the window, draw the curtain to look at the snow outside, sigh a little bit, then come downstage center, sit in the armchair, and then begin to speak." The ingenue said with the greatest humility, "Would you mind—don't you think I am holding up the action of the play? Would you mind if I just came onstage, sat in the armchair, and started to speak right away?" Ethel Barrymore said, "Of course, my dear, if you feel more comfortable that way—why not?" Came time for the ingenue's exit and again Miss B. said, "Now, my child, it is time for you to make your exit, and I would go up to the piano, maybe strike a note or two, think that the pictures on the piano need dusting, look at your father's picture, sigh a little, and then make your exit." The ingenue again said, with the greatest humility, "Forgive me, Miss Barrymore, but don't you think it would be redundant? Don't you think the scene is over and that, if you don't mind, it would be much better if I just walked offstage?" Again Miss Barrymore said, "Of course, my dear, anything to make you happy." With that Miss B. walked up on the stage, went over to the stage manager, and said, "Who is that sweet unspoiled child? It's a shame she won't be with us after lunch."

BEAUMONT, BINKIE

Right after World War II I was in the South of France and I was going to dine *à trois* with two English friends of mine, both in the theater. They called and asked if Binkie could join us for dinner. I was still an actor and, of course, I was thrilled. The three of them joined me on the terrace of the Carlton. Binkie sat down and never addressed a word to me. He spoke about Ian and Noël and Donald and Peter—all of whom I knew, but he didn't know that. We went on to dinner. Still not a word. Then on to the casino. My two friends were not gambling—at that time the English were allowed to take only a very small amount of money out of their country. Binkie sat down next to me and my pile of chips kept growing and his kept diminishing. Finally he turned to me and for the first time spoke: "I say, old boy, could you let me have some money? Of course, you know who I am." I said, "Yes, I do know who you are; you are one of the rudest men I have ever met." He left the casino in a huff and I never saw him after that— I also never worked for him.

BEEBE, LUCIUS

Before any of the nonsense about being gay or not being gay, he used to go to first nights in full evening dress—white tie and tails and a high hat. With a sailor.

BEHRMAN, S. N.

We met on the *Queen Elizabeth* sailing to New York. I begged him to tell me some of his marvelous stories about the Lunts et al. He did tell me one about Noël. When he was at the peak of his career with plays running on both sides of the Atlantic, Noël was playing in *This Year of Grace* and having a ball, enjoying every moment of his success. S. N. used to sit in his dressing room every night and wait for all of his *bons mots*. One night there was a minor English actress sitting in Noël's dressing room while he was making up. She was going on and on about all her troubles—no money, bad road tours—she never stopped grumbling. Noël was not a patient man and he was getting more exasperated by the minute. At last he looked at her and said, "And let's face it, Gladys, you're not getting any younger."

When we ended our five-day voyage I was very flattered because Behrman (who was a very private person) gave me his phone number and said to please call him. "I really mean it," he said, "but don't call me before noon." I assumed he liked to sleep late, but I was inquisitive and asked him why, and he said, "I am always terrified it is going to be Irene Selznick."

BELMONT, AUGUST

The story goes that he was walking in front of Saint Patrick's Cathedral one day with a midget and he said, "That's my church—I used to be a Jew," and the midget said, "I used to be short!"

BENNET, CONSTANCE

Dining at Michael's Pub one night I was introduced to Constance Bennet. I said I remembered her in a film called *Sons of the Gods* with Richard Barthelmes. She played a society girl who has an affair with Richard Barthelmes and finds out that he has Chinese blood. There was a wonderful scene in which she comes into a beautiful drawing room, looking fantastic in riding clothes, and beats him with her riding crop. Constance (who hated being called Connie) said, "You couldn't possibly have seen that film. How old are you?" I said I was forty-five and she said, "We're the same age," which meant that she was twelve years old when she made the film.

BERNSTEIN, LEONARD (LENNY)

What can I say about him? Aside from anything else, his sister, Shirley, is my good friend and agent. In *On the Town* he used to come onstage and sit in the nightclub scene. I played the M.C., and when he wasn't there I would get a big laugh on some bit of business that I used to do. When he was there he used to laugh before the fact and kill the laugh. I almost hit him one night and he stopped.

Right after we opened and were a big hit, two other singers and myself went on the *Kate Smith Show* on radio to sing "New York, New York—It's a Helluva Town" with Lenny conducting the orchestra. Kate Smith kept singing and singing "God Bless America," which we all know and love, but enough is enough.

At that time one couldn't say "hell" on the radio (hard to believe). At any rate, there we were, exhausted from sitting around all day with no rehearsal and we were on the air. Lenny played the intro and forgot to bring in the three singers at the right second. I picked it up, he looked at me with a great sigh of relief, and I became so smug that I forgot and sang, "New York, New York—It's a Helluva Town." Needless to say, I never worked for Kate Smith again.

Lenny, as we all know, kisses everybody, but as opposed to most people in show business, he really means it.

BISMARK, COUNTESS MONA

Countess Mona Bismark was probably one of the most chic women who ever lived. Romney Brent told me the story—and I do hope it is true—that she was on a cruise and the ship stopped in Israel. She got off the boat dressed in a beautiful blue chiffon dress, with a beautiful chiffon parasol. Looking like a dream with her magnificent blue eyes and white hair, she went for a stroll with Romney and came to the Wailing Wall. There was one little old Jewish woman weeping and wailing and pounding the wall. As Mona passed, the little old Jewish woman took one look at this magnificent creature and started wailing and beating the wall even harder.

BOOTH, SHIRLEY

I used to see her at Leonard Sillman's parties and I can remember only one thing about her: she was offered *Auntie Mame* when it was a play and she turned it down because there were too many costume changes.

BOYNE, EVA LEONARD

A minor actress who played a maid in *The Chalk Garden*. She was terribly grand and played the part with a monocle. She got to be a certain age and decided she had paid her dues and was tired of living in a tacky hotel on Forty-fifth Street, so she applied to the Actor's House and was accepted. She packed and took the train and arrived rather late in the evening. She unpacked her bag and got into full evening dress, plus the monocle, and came downstairs. There was one little cleaning man there and she asked, "Where's the bar?" He said, "Bar? We ain't got no bar." She pulled herself up to her haughtiest pose and said, "No bar," went upstairs, packed, and took the next train back to New York.

BROWNE, CORAL

An absolute darling and a very skillful actress, but has a lashing tongue, I am told.

She is now married to Vincent Price, but she was married before to another actor, and she was in rehearsal with a production of *Macbeth*, playing Lady Macbeth. In her contract, her husband was supposed to have a part in the production, but she noticed the first morning that there was nothing in the play for him. So she went over to the stage manager and said, "Where's my husband's part?" The stage manager said that there was nothing in the play that he was right for—that there was no part. She said in a very commanding voice, "I'll find him a part," and she looked through the play. Finally her index finger pointed to a page in the text. The stage manager looked where she was pointing and saw a description of the scene: "A deserted camp."

☆

Radie Harris writes a column for the Hollywood *Reporter*. She adores England and the English, and she keeps going back and forth between London and New York, which is a bit of a struggle because the poor woman has a wooden leg.

She wrote something unpleasant about Coral in her column one day. Sometime later, she was spending the summer in England and went to a restaurant for supper one night after the theater. She was seated at a table with a friend and along came Coral Browne, who went up to her, gave her a big kiss, and said, "Radie, darling, I hear the whole of London is at your foot."

BURTON, RICHARD

When Richard Burton (who couldn't have been nicer) came over to America to rehearse in *Equus*, I thought as one of the producers I should go to greet him at the theater. I arrived a moment too late and he was going through the play with the stage manager. I waited in the wings because I didn't want to disturb him. I thought to myself, That glorious voice is still there and he seems to know his lines. At the very end of the play, when the boy is exorcized or saved or whatever, the doctor walks around the arena and says something to the effect, "Who knows, one day you may even find this funny—smirky funny—you may even find your private parts funny." Anyway, Richard went through everything to the end saying, "Who knows, one day you may even find your, your . . ." and forgot "private parts."

Before Burton opened in *Equus*, John Dexter wisely decided to put him on at a matinee. When the stage manager announced that he would be playing the matinee, the audience went mad. The cheering and the applause were tremendous.

When he came out onstage he had his hands in his pockets and kept them there for the entire performance. He forgot most of his lines and really gave a terrible performance. Came time for the bows and the hand was very polite for him but the boy got a standing ovation.

He went back to his dressing room and thought, This will never do.

That evening he gave the same performance, except at the end of the play he took his hands out of his pockets and ranted and raved and flung his arms about as though he were in *Macbeth*. It had nothing to do with *Equus*, and the audience rose in one second and cheered and cheered and cheered. I shouldn't grumble, because it did put some money in my pocket, and he turned the play into a three-year instead of a one-year run.

His *Hamlet*, directed and miscast by John Gielgud, was a huge success and the "in thing" to see. The night I saw it a woman sat next to me and the moment the curtain went up she fell sound asleep and slept through the entire production. When the curtain finally came down she rose to her feet and shouted, "Bravo, bravo."

CAERNARVON, EARL OF

Having lunch with the Earl of Caernarvon (Porchy) in his glorious house at Highclere is a mélange of the most wonderful furniture, paintings, porcelain—and tinned spaghetti with paper napkins!

CALHERN, LOU

He was a very good actor who also lived at the Elysee. I knew him only slightly. He was very tall and had a terrific drinking problem. On occasion I would see him running up and down the hall stark naked, looking like a rather chic Ichabod Crane.

CALLAS, MARIA

The best actress I have ever seen, other than Laurette Taylor.

CAPOTE, TRUMAN

He told me that he hated to go home because his mother used to call all her friends and say, "Come on over, Truman's back."

CANTOR, EDDIE

Some years ago in Capri, it took me two hours to dress at the Quisisana Hotel. I couldn't decide on my sandals and my sport shirt and my shorts. Finally I emerged from the hotel and walked very slowly to the piazza. On the way, I kept seeing reflections of myself in shop windows and thought: "You look marvelous." I sat down in the piazza with Baron Barracco, ordered a Cinzano, and with the Mediterranean breezes blowing, I was feeling very grand indeed. Suddenly a young Italian contessa came over to the table (a friend of the Baron) and Stano asked her to join the table. She kept staring at me and I wondered what she was looking at. Then she said, "You look like a movie star." I suddenly thought of Cary Grant. She hesitated a moment and then said, "Eddie Cantor." I went back to the Quisisana and didn't leave my room for three days. One consolation: Cole Porter was mistaken for Eddie Cantor, too!

CAVALLI, CONTESSA

She comes to Barbados every winter and somebody once asked her what she thought was rich and she said, "$100,000,000 and I am very rich."

CHAMPION, GOWER

I auditioned for a musical called *Small Wonder*. Gower Champion flew up onstage after I had passed the singing part of my audition and grabbed my hand and said, "Do this." He did a few tippy taps, which I copied, and he said, "Marvelous." I didn't get the job, but I still remember the steps.

CHANNING, CAROL

I toured with Carol Channing in *Gentlemen Prefer Blondes* for a season. As everybody knows, she never misses a performance. Aside from being a great trouper in the old tradition, she is a Christian Scientist. We got to Boston, where her father is one of the heads of the Mother Church, and I was invited to the house for dinner. I couldn't care less about drinking, but when I *can't* have something I go mad. So I poured some gin into a tiny medicine bottle and about fifteen minutes before dinner was served I asked my host for some ginger ale, sneaked into the bathroom, and poured some gin in the glass. I then proceeded to relax and have a lovely evening.

CHURCHILL, LORD CHARLES SPENCER

He was brought to lunch at the Berkeley in London by a friend of mine. (He had not been invited.) There is a lovely restaurant in the hotel called The Perroquet, which has a magnificent buffet table from which I chose my lunch. He paid no attention and ordered a most sumptuous meal with white wine, red wine, brandy, and cigars. I paid the bill. Three days later he rang me up and said, "I say, old boy, what a lovely lunch we had. Couldn't we do the same thing today?" I said, "I would love to, where are you taking me?" Suddenly he was too busy, and I never saw him again.

CLAIRE, INA

Gertrude Lawrence gave a New Year's Eve party at the Mark Hopkins Hotel in San Francisco in 1947 for the cast of *Tonight at 8:30,* and the only outsiders were Ina Claire and her husband. She arrived late with a dozen American beauty roses in her arms, gave them to G. L., and told her to put them in water right away, as though she were talking to the maid. Then she sat down and never stopped talking for the next four hours. At one moment she suddenly got thirsty. As she reached for her drink and put it to her lips, I started to say something. She put her hand over my mouth, took a sip, and went right on talking.

At midnight a Scottish bagpiper came down the hall and we followed him to the lobby of the Mark Hopkins. I found myself doing a Scottish fling with both Gertrude Lawrence and Ina Claire. Somebody said I should have died after that—and perhaps he was right.

☆

At the Berkeley in London one night, just a few years ago (Ina Claire was somewhere in her nineties), she gave a dinner in the main, mauve dining room. She seated everybody and then suddenly looked up to see the way the light was hitting her and said, "Up, everybody" and changed the whole seating.

CLIFT, MONTGOMERY

I met him only twice in my life. The first time was in a subway while I was in *On the Town*. He couldn't have been nicer. He came up to me and told me he thought I was wonderful in the show. This was quite a compliment, as I was doing only bits and pieces.

The next time I saw him was at Nancy Walker's apartment and he was a mess. I lost all patience with him and *told* him he was a mess and that any actor in New York would give his back teeth to have one-tenth of his gifts and that he was throwing them all away. It didn't help.

COCHRANE, LADY

Sir Charles's wife. She was an alcoholic and was talked into going to a doctor about her drinking. He suggested that instead of drinking she should eat an apple and she replied, "Doctor, I can't eat forty-seven apples a day."

COLBERT, CLAUDETTE

Claudette is a terrific swimmer (I swim with her all the time in Barbados). Her backstroke is better than Eleanor Holmes's. She is a wonderful hostess. The food in her beautiful house in Barbados is perfect and little peals of laughter always echo from her porch or her beach or her drawing room, decorated with pictures of President Reagan and the Pope. She is very, very bright. I have known her for almost twenty years, and aside from the fact that she looks at the most forty-four, she is the cleanest woman I have ever known.

Her energy is boundless. She never wants to go to bed. In New York one night, I took her to see *Bedroom Farce*, and I asked her if she would mind having her picture taken with the cast after the play, as it would be good publicity for the show. She said that she didn't do that sort of thing, but she would do it for me. I asked her not to do it just for me, but she insisted.

After the play we went backstage. There was a photographer there and she said, "What's that?" I turned to the photographer and said, "Forget it." She tugged my sleeve and said that she had promised; I told her to forget it and again she insisted. Finally she had her picture taken and off we went to my flat to have some supper.

We sat up until about 2:00 a.m. talking and laughing and bubbling. Being with her is like drinking a glass of champagne. I finally took her home, gave her a delicious, big kiss, and said goodnight. Her parting line to me was, "Don't send that picture out until I have seen it."

When I called the publicity man in the morning to tell him not to send the picture out until I had seen it, he told me that it had already gone out.

When I don't know what to do—I don't do anything. Please, Claudette, once and for all, it had gone out before I could stop it.

Noël did a production of *Blithe Spirit* for television, and he was having a very rough time with Claudette. Finally he looked at her and said, "Claudette, *if* you had a neck, I'd wring it." As she tells the story on herself, I don't think she would mind if I put it into print.

Claudette's feud with Verna Hull on Barbados added a certain amount of tension to holidays. The whole thing is a shame because Verna and Claudette used to be the greatest of friends. They had a terrible *crise,* Claudette built a wall, and the island was divided in half. One was either a friend of Verna or a friend of Claudette. I have managed to be a friend of both and I hope to remain that. The feud had its amusing sides. I really don't know if they were competing, but Verna would have all the Royals, from Princess Margaret on down, and Claudette would have all the show folk, from Frank Sinatra on down. When we went into the sea at Verna's, Princess Margaret used to lead the way when she was still married to Lord Snowden, then Oliver Messell, his uncle, then Verna, then me.

On the other side, Claudette would lead the way, followed by Frank Sinatra and a group of show folk. All very Fellini.

We were all paddling about on the sea, chattering away like a pack of chipmunks, when P. M. announced that she was going to swim over to say hello to Claudette. Verna said, "Help yourself ma'am." She paddled over and was gossiping away and in about fifteen minutes she came back and said that the whole feud was silly—that it was rather like the upstairs maid and the second butler getting a divorce.

COOPER, GLADYS

I went to the first night in New York of *Edward My Son*, starring Robert Morley with the most brilliant performance by Peggy Ashcroft. There was a party afterward at The Blue Angel in honor of Mr. Morley. About fourteen of us were at table for supper and Miss Cooper seated everybody and became the hostess (she was Mr. Morley's mother-in-law). Robert Morley was forgotten, Peggy Ashcroft was forgotten, and so was everybody else at table. Gladys Cooper was the star and somehow it was right.

She had a sister who was a minor actress who had decided to give it up because she kept hearing hissing noises every time she came out on stage. But finally a friend told her that the audience was just saying, "That's Gladys Cooper's sister."

CORNELL, KATHERINE

I first saw her in Martha's Vineyard where she had a summer home. I was working at the theater in Oak Bluffs. She used to drive over in her station wagon in jeans, looking glorious. But every time she would slam the door of the car I was sure it was going to break. I also remember her theatrical office, where I used to go when I was making the rounds. She had two of the largest Doberman pinschers I have ever seen, which terrified me. She hired an actor for *The Barretts of Wimpole Street* simply because he had an adorable cocker spaniel to play Flush.

COWARD, NOEL

Where do I begin? Do I start at age fifteen, when I first heard a recording of "Let's Say Goodbye" which I subsequently played five thousand times? Or do I begin in 1947, when I met Noël at my dentist's (who had the silly name of Dr. Sandman)? Or do I discuss the lunch I had at Les Avants in Switzerland with him and Kay Thompson, or the week that Noël was in Capri? There was that long tour across America with Gertrude Lawrence, and Christmas on the train, with Gee giving presents to the whole cast—a lovely ostrich cigarette case for me. Noël joined us in Baltimore, Princeton, and San Francisco (where I was understudying seventeen parts and everybody got sick at once). No, I won't go into any of that; but I will try to tell a few stories that I don't think are in print.

Noël was sitting in a little restaurant on Fire Island, of all places, when an elderly lady came up to him shaking and asked whether he was Noël Coward. He snapped back, "Yes, I am," and she said, "My husband thought so." Then Noël said, "I saw him think it."

Noël was at a party, and sitting at the far end of the room was a young actor. Noël asked what his name was and somebody said Keir Dullea; and without missing a beat Noël said, "Gone tomorrow."

Noël had been having some tax problems in America, and Leonard Sillman suggested he call his lawyer. Noël asked Leonard his lawyer's name and when Leonard said Max Chopnick, Noël, again without missing a beat, said, "Chop as in chop, and Nick as in Nick?"

☆

By now everybody knows the story of the Queen of Tonga on the occasion of the coronation of Queen Elizabeth II. The crowd went mad about her. She was enormous and drove in a large open carriage with a black driver and a little black man sitting opposite her. Noël was watching the procession from a balcony with some of his friends when somebody asked: "Who is that little black man sitting with the Queen in her carriage?" Noël replied, "I really don't know—probably her lunch."

☆

Noël went to see the musical version of *Gone With the Wind*. A great friend of mine, Kenneth Carter, who died some years ago, was an agent who adored old-time movie stars, among them Bessie Love, who played Aunt Pittypat. Unfortunately, you couldn't hear a word she said. Kenneth was talking to Noël over the phone and asked him how he liked Bessie Love. Noël said, "The best thing in it." Kenneth asked, "Could you hear her?" Noël said, "Not a word, which is more than I can say for the rest of the cast." Kenneth then asked him how he liked the whole show and Noël said, "I'll tell you, if they had taken that terrible child in the second act and shoved him up the ass of the horse in the first act, they might have had something!"

Noël was being interviewed on television one night and the interviewer asked him what he did at night to relax. Noël replied, "I'm not going to tell you with all these people watching me!"

Noël did an Australian tour many years ago and hated every minute of it. At the end of the tour some idiotic newspaperman said, "I hear you're funny, say something funny," and Noël said, "Kangaroo."

When I auditioned for Noël in 1947, I felt I was auditioning for Jesus Christ. Anyway, I sang and danced for him and then he came up onstage and we read a scene from *Red Peppers*. When I had finished he said, "You are a very good actor. I adore the way you sing. You move terribly well, and you have the best Cockney accent I have ever heard on an American. However, you are veddy, veddy short. Can you wear Adler elevators?" I said yes, but I had them on. I was as tall as I was going to get.

We did six of Noël's original nine one-act plays in the 1947 revival of *Tonight at 8:30*. The first three plays opened and the critics hated everything about them. We all had to go to the theater and rehearse that day before opening the second set. Noël was sitting hunched up, hidden in his camel's hair coat and hat, while the cast rehearsed *Fumed Oak*. There is a scene where the father (played by Philip Tonge) has to slap his mother (played by Norah Howard) in the face, and as I came down the aisle the first word out of Noël was "harder." They went back to start the scene again from the top. When they got to the same face-slapping moment, Noël, again without looking up, said, *"Still* harder." Norah then stepped forward and said, "Noël, do you want me to open tonight?" and Noël said, "Dimly."

After the second set of dreadful notices, Noël was undaunted and called the cast onstage and said, "To hell with them," meaning the critics. "Gertie, you're divine, we are all divine, and anyway they adored us in Newark."

When Noël was playing in London in *Suite in Three Keys* I went to the matinee and Noël said afterward, "You must tell me about my American accent, as I listen to Henry Fonda records before going on." His accent was based on an old friend named Edward Barber, who owned a steamship company and once loaned Noël fifty dollars when he was about seventeen years old and broke in New York. At any rate, Noël came onstage with a red wig, dragging a set of golf clubs, and kept saying, "yup" and "nope." Suddenly the telephone rang and Noël picked it up and said in clipped British tones, "Hallo."

Poor divine Beatrice Lillie is now without memory. The last musical she did in New York was *High Spirits*, based on Noël's second-best play, *Blithe Spirit*. She had a terrible time learning her lines. When they opened in Boston Noël was there. Somebody ran up to him and said, "Isn't it wonderful, Bea remembered all her lines," and Noël said, "All but 127 of them."

Noël had a lifelong friend who became his business manager. Unfortunately, he also became a drunk rather late in life. Noël (who had no patience) went to visit him and said, "I want you to do me a favor, either drink yourself to death very quickly or stop, because you are boring everybody to death." I think that is the best advice one can give an alcoholic.

I was at a party that was given for Noël one night in Leonard Sillman's apartment. He had about twenty people, and when Noël arrived everybody shut up and became very self-conscious, including Noël. Finally Imogene Coca arrived with an enormous black poodle who went over to Noël, turned his back on him, squatted, and broke wind that could be heard six blocks away. Noël looked down at the dog and said, "After all, I did write *Cavalcade.*"

COWLES, FLEUR

I have never been to Fleur's flat in London, but I have had lunch at her glorious house in the country. As a matter of fact she has two houses: first you have cocktails in one, and then you walk in the rain with servants and umbrellas to the other house (all very Felliniesque). Everything that is served is grown on her land. She seemed very distracted and did nothing but paint during cocktails, lunch, and coffee.

CRAIG, DAVID

David is the husband of Nancy Walker, and both are very dear old friends. I was in *On the Town* with Nancy and I used David in a quartet in an Equity Library Theatre production of *Pal Joey,* of which I was the producer. He is the best coach for actresses who cannot sing, and he has helped Alexis Smith, Angela Lansbury, Jean Simmons, and many others. Every turn of the head, movement of the hand, and look up to the balcony are David Craig on the stage. I know because I studied with him, too. He also has a famous biting tongue and I have made a collection of his remarks through the years: "Who needs the Lunts?" "Is Oscar Hammerstein kidding?" "Mary

Martin is a stage wait," and "Dick Rodgers has been getting away with murder for years." When Nancy and David went to London for the first time I was dying to know their reaction. The minute they got back to New York I called them and asked, "What did you think of London?" David said, "What's all that polite shit?"

CUEVAS, MARQUESA DE

I took the Marquesa (who is the granddaughter of John D. Rockefeller) to the casino in Cannes one night. She was worried that since she did not have her passport with her she would not be allowed in the casino. I assured her that there would be no problem. When she entered, the entire staff bowed, hoping to get some of her hard-earned loot. We sat down at the same roulette table and I asked her if I could play the same numbers she played. (She had to win and did and never stopped.) My chips were worth four times hers, and I won along with her. Suddenly she got bored or thrifty and said: "I will wait for you in the bar." I was greedy and stayed on and, of course, the minute she left the table I gave back every penny.

The Marquesa is always late, late, late. I crossed on the *Queen Elizabeth* and a friend of mine called to ask me to look after the Marquesa while I was on the ship. The first evening I called her and asked her if she would like to join me and some friends in the smoking room before dinner. She thanked me very kindly but said she was unpacking and would I please call her tomorrow, which I did. She said she was still unpacking. By the time she had finished unpacking she was starting to pack again, so she never met us for drinks.

She had a faithful servant called Marcel. Once she was about to take a train from Cannes to Paris and kept running from bag to bag, trying to organize her luggage, while Marcel stood at dutiful attention. Suddenly she looked at her watch, knew she was going to be late, and said, "Marcel, go stand in front of the train!"

DALI, SALVADOR

Salvador Dali and I crossed on the *QE II* and the only thing I can remember about him is that he never changed his clothes.

DALRYMPLE, JEAN

Jean is a producer, once married to José Iturbi. Rumor has it that he used to drag her by her hair, which is very long. She has been around for years and years and years, and she always looks exactly the same. What does she do? I saw her one night at an Off-Broadway opening, when she came in late. She sat down next to me and I hissed at her. She said she was sorry, but her husband was ill. So I apologized profusely and she said, "Well, he isn't dead!"

DAVIS, BETTE

At a New Year's Eve party, Kaye Ballard introduced us. Frankly, I was slightly nervous. However, from about 9:00 p.m. until 3:00 a.m. we never stopped talking. We loved the same things and we also hated the same things. At about 1:00 a.m. in New York I walked her home in a blizzard. She asked me to come in so she could make me some scrambled eggs (can't spell it the way she pronounced it!). She flew up the stairs to change into a pair of slacks, leaving me to wait nervously in my dinner jacket in the kitchen with a Siamese cat (which terrified me). She came back and scrambled the eggs *à la* Bette Davis and we talked long into the night. When I left it was still snowing. I don't know whether this really happened or if the whole evening was just out of a Bette Davis movie.

She was once very ill during a newspaper strike and a rumor went around that she had died. An old friend called her up and asked her about the rumor and she said, "You don't think I would die during a newspaper strike, do you?"

DEMILLE, AGNES

The choreographer directed *Out of This World* before George Abbott came in to fix things up. The first day of rehearsal she gathered the cast together and said, "I hope you all believe in the Greek gods." Right away I knew that we, the show, and Agnes were in trouble.

DEMPSEY, JACK

When I was about seventeen years old and weighed about seventeen pounds, I was at a nightclub in New York and got quite drunk one night and went up to Jack Dempsey and said, "You're not so tough." He leaned over and kissed me.

DEXTER, JOHN

Ever since *Equus*, Mr. Dexter, who was the director, and I have had a running gag. As the English say, we are "not on speakers." Wherever we are, be it Sardi's in New York or the Savoy Grill in London, our eyes meet, we stare at each other, never say hello, never nod, never in any way let on that we know each other. However, at the opening of the revival of *Fiddler on the Roof*, starring Zero Mostel, at the Winter Garden in New York, we walked into the theater during the interval at the same moment. He forgot and said, "Hello." I didn't and smugly walked into the theater. I had won.

DIETRICH, MARLENE

At Leo Lehrman's house, Miss Dietrich arrived in a blue velvet jacket and black velvet slacks, with a pot roast under her arm. The most glamorous looking woman I had ever seen.

Some years later, Montgomery Clift, Roddy McDowall, Nancy Walker, and her husband, David Craig, used to meet at Monty's house once a week for dinner. One night Roddy said, "For God's sake, Monty, you are a big movie star, you can have anybody here you want. Why don't you ask somebody more interesting than we are?" He called Noël—who accepted right away. Then he called Miss Dietrich and left a message with her answering service to say that Monty had called. She thought he meant Field Marshal Montgomery. Nevertheless, she was at Monty Clift's house with Roddy and David and Nancy and Noël the following week. During the evening David Craig cornered Marlene and told her that Nancy was about to do a nightclub act and that, although she was very comfortable on the stage and was used to the cinema, she was a nervous wreck about appearing in a nightclub. He asked her how she coped with nerves. She said that it couldn't be easier. "I sit in my dressing room, put on my makeup, get into my dress, and fix my hair. The stage manager says, 'You're on, Miss Dietrich.' I take a last look in the mirror and see the most beautiful woman in the world and make my entrance. Why would I be nervous?"

I did a television show with her daughter, Maria Riva. She was funny about her mother. She said that if she earned $100,000 a year she would spend $100,000 a year on clothes, never thinking she had to pay for anything else. Maria told me that when she was a young girl she was very fat and not at all attractive. Her mother took her over to a long mirror and said, "You look awful and I looked the same way when I was your age. Now look at what you are going to look like."

DORSAY, FIFI

Jack Arnold, who used to play the piano in the Monkey Bar of the Elysee Hotel, was an old friend of Miss Dorsay and he told me that she rather liked sex. One day he ran into the French actress on Fifth Avenue and she said, "Oh, Arnold, I have discovered the vibrator — now I don't have to talk to anybody."

DRAKE, ALFRED

Alfred told me that when *Kean* (a musical) opened in New York, Brooks Atkinson, then the critic for *The New York Times*, wrote, "*Kean* is *almost* a perfect musical." The word "almost" in *The New York Times* destroyed any chance of its being a success.

DUKE, VERNON

Born Vladimir Duelsky, he liked very fat women for some odd reason. He couldn't have been nicer to me. In Paris he took me to Yves Montand's debut (sensational) and one night we went to see Louis Jouvet in *Ondine.* Jouvet took forever and by the time he pronounced the word *Ondine,* four hours had gone by. Vernon was born in Russia but was raised in Paris and spoke perfect French. My high-school French was awful, and at the curtain I said that I hadn't understood one word anybody said and Vernon, yawning, replied, "Neither did I."

EGGERT, MARTHA

She was doing a revival of *The Merry Widow* in New York, starring Jan Kipura and produced by a mid-European called Yolande Mirion. They were rehearsing and Yolande's secretary was taking notes when she heard Miss Eggert singing "Vilia, oh Vilia, the Vitch of the Voods." Later that day the secretary was going through her notes with Miss Mirion and told her that Miss Eggert was singing "Vilia, oh Vilia, the Vitch of the Voods" and Miss Mirion said "Vell?"

ERTE

The big question is: Does he have a first name? It is true that he is over ninety, but I must say he looks it. We go walking on the beach all the time in Barbados. He laughs a lot. He is quite incredible and has enormous talent, but I still don't know whether he really understands English.

FERRER, JOSE

Herman Levin told me that they couldn't find a leading man for *The Girl Who Came to Supper*, Noël Coward's version of Terence Rattigan's *The Sleeping Prince*. They auditioned and auditioned and Herman merely suggested José Ferrer to Noël and Noël snapped back, "He's too short." They went on and on searching when finally, out of desperation, Herman again mentioned José Ferrer and Noël surprisingly enough said, "Very well. Fly him in from the coast." José Ferrer had a very big voice and he came onstage and sang "Were Thine That Special Face" from *Kiss Me Kate* and Noël hissed in Herman's ear, "That's our boy." They were having a drink about an hour later and Herman became curious and said to Noël, "What made you change your mind when you had said he's too short?" Noël thought for a minute and said, "Oh, I must have been thinking of Toulouse-Lautrec." The only time he had ever seen José Ferrer was in *Moulin Rouge* and he thought that was how tall he was.

FLANAGAN & ALLEN & NERVO & KNOX

were very funny English comics (like Olsen and Johnson in *Hellzapoppin*). One of them was supposed to be a dirty old man who liked young virgins to talk dirty to him while he was at it. One night he found one very young virgin, got her into the sack, and while they were making love he looked at her and said, "What am I doing to you?" She looked up with her innocent little eyes and said, "You're hurting me, Mr. Flanagan or Allen or Nervo or Knox."

FOCH, NINA

Nina had a mother by the name of Consuelo Flowerton, who was very beautiful and was in the Ziegfeld Follies of 1918. Consuelo had a very minor talent but had to earn a living in order to bring up her daughter. She got a nightclub act together and worked, as she used to say, "in saloons." She also had a lot of energy and had to use it up somehow. One of the things she did was study the violin. She studied and studied and studied. After about five years her teacher said she had studied enough and she should go out and get a job. She did—at Chin Lee's on Broadway and something like Forty-fifth Street. (She had to start somewhere.) She was supposed to do about eight shows a day, the first one at 11:00 a.m. She fiddled on her fiddle for fifteen minutes and then, having launched her new career, went back to her dressing room to wait for the next show. Suddenly there was a knock on the door and a very small Chinese waiter poked his head in and said, "Missy, you no go on for second show."

FONTAINE, JOAN

Joan called me up one day and said she thought we should get married; but she couldn't decide if she would be called Joan Milton or I would be called Frank Fontaine. Anyway, I told her that it would be an impossible match as I loved to play bridge and she didn't play at all. She said, "Okay. On the nights you play bridge, I'll go bowling."

FONTANNE, LYNN

Went on and on and on, and was incredible. She is the only woman in history who gained twenty pounds and became glamorous. A friend of mine, Leonard Speigelgass, who wrote *A Majority of One,* told me that he spent a weekend with her and her husband, Alfred Lunt, and she did nothing but talk about money, surrounded by the most beautiful furniture, porcelain, and servants. Leonard suggested that she seemed to have enough money and she said, "Oh, I don't mean my kind of money—I mean Onassis's kind of money."

☆

When she was young and just married to Alfred Lunt, they decided they would become stars, each individually, and then come together. She became a star overnight in a play called *Dulcy* and he in Booth Tarkington's *Clarence*. Then they came together — never to part. Years and years went by and many, many hits. Neither one of them left the other's side or missed a performance — a true love match.

Finally one night he got sick and was carted off to the hospital and had to miss a performance. She went on without him and finally the curtain came down. As she walked offstage and passed the stage manager, she said, "How was I?"

Montgomery Clift told me that when he was the juvenile lead in *There Shall Be No Night* Lynn used to have a card table in the wings so she could relax with a game of solitaire until she had to go back onstage. When she wasn't acting she did nothing but relax and rest, and Monty said that he was convinced that she didn't know that there was a thing called World War II.

Two little matinee ladies went to see her in a play. One of them had seen her before and the other had never seen her. When the curtain came down the one who had seen her said, "Isn't she marvelous and did you ever see such beautiful hands?" The lady who hadn't seen her before said, "Yes, but are they hers?"

There is another story of two matinee ladies, one who had seen the Lunts before and one who had not. When the curtain came down, the one who had seen them said, "Aren't they marvelous?" and the one who had never seen them said, "Yes, but I always thought there were three of them."

FONTEYN, DAME MARGOT

The magnificent ballerina was introduced to me by my great friends Turnbull Barton and John McHugh, who used to entertain the near great, the great, and the not so great in their lovely Manhattan town house. They asked me to take Dame Margot to see *A Chorus Line* when it was still playing Off-Broadway. When it was over she said, "If I had had to do that nobody would ever have heard of me."

Tug and John asked me to take her home one night from one of their many dinners. In the taxi she sighed and said, "Oh, how I wish I could take a long holiday." I have never seen anybody look so tired as she did when she said that to me.

FOSSE, BOB

I used to audition and audition for him and he always used to come running down the aisle and up onstage and tell me how great I was and then would say, "If only there was something in the show for you."

FRASER (PINTER), LADY ANTONIA

Spending time with Antonia is always a joy. Aside from her beauty and brilliance she has the most wonderful sense of humor. We were dining in Barbados with Jonathan Aitken and Verna Hull, a great friend of mine, when Verna said, "I adore Frank. He always gets me out of last-minute dates that I didn't want to make in the first place." Antonia was immediately on to a game. "Very well," she said, "I am giving a dinner in Verna's honor. It has been planned for a year. Eighteen people to a sit-down dinner, black tie, the lot. Get her out of that one at the last minute." I said, "Ting-a-ling." Antonia picked up an imaginary telephone and I said, "Antonia, I have terrible news for you. Verna passed away this morning!"

I gave a dinner at the Berkeley in London for Antonia. Afterward, eight of us went upstairs to my tiny room and watched Antonia on television, something about Scotland. All of us were lying on the bed as there was no room to sit down. The next day she sent a thank-you note: "As for the TV, well I always think all parties should end up in the bedroom, don't you?"

She is one of the great sleepers of the twentieth century. How she manages to do everything she does is a wonderment—between the books and the children and the husbands—but she manages to fall asleep even at *Chorus Line,* until one moment she woke up with all that banging about and said to Harold Pinter with great hope in her voice, "Is it over?"

She also is a brave lady. She was staying with Janet Kidd in Barbados some years ago and in the middle of the night she suddenly realized that she had left her diary in the living room. When she crept downstairs, one of the guard dogs that had been let loose to protect the house was standing next to her diary, but on she went, grabbed the book, and calmly walked back to her bedroom with the guard dog staring at her in amazement.

Antonia told me that she was flying from Rome to London with a woman who was terrified of flying. They were about halfway when that awful little click went on and you knew the captain was going to say, "Something terrible . . ." He announced that something was wrong with one of the engines and that they had to turn back to Rome. The woman started to scream and yell and carry on and Antonia, to calm her down, handed her a newspaper and said firmly,

"Here, read this." The woman grabbed the paper and looked at the headline. It read in big, bold letters: PLANE CRASH OFF THE ITALIAN COAST.

FURNESS, BETTY

I met Betty in Rome at least twenty-five years ago, only once, and I am amazed (and delighted) that when she sees me on Madison Avenue, or wherever, she always says, "Hello, Frank."

GAINES, GEORGE

One night during the run of Cole Porter's *Out of This World* George Gaines (who was playing Jupiter) was onstage looking very handsome in a long white flowing gown and a long white flowing beard. He was standing on a large platform, with a wind machine behind him blowing everything in sight. I was in the wings with one of the dancers, who said, "He looks just like a cheap lamp."

GARBO, GRETA

I came out of a restaurant in New York and saw Garbo. I was with a relative and I grabbed his arm and said, "Oh, my God, there's Greta Garbo"; he said, "She's a dog." The next morning I called my attorney and took him out of my will.

GERRERA, REYNALDO

I sometimes think I would like to write a book about the very rich and call it *Guillotine Stories*. One of them would be the story that Reynaldo told me about his grandfather, who had never done a day's work in his life and was summoned to jury duty and couldn't get out of it.

He was a very late riser and for his first morning in court the butler shook him, the maid brought him a wet cloth to wake him up, and the cook brought his orange juice and coffee in bed. The butler dressed him and they brought him down to the street and got him into the limousine. As he was being pulled away, he looked at everybody on the street going about their morning business and said to the chauffeur, "Are all these people going to jury duty?"

GIELGUD, JOHN

There are endless stories about Sir John's mistakes on purpose.

He has a way of sneaking in an opinion and then getting out of it. Somebody suggested Laurence Olivier for a certain role and Sir John said, "He's dead. I mean, he's veddy, veddy ill. I mean he isn't well at all." Vivien Leigh came to see him during World War II and suggested a certain play to do to entertain the troops, and he said, "But you can't act—I mean you are wrong for the part—I mean the troops won't like it at all."

There is an actress in the theater named Margalo Gillmore; in London the same story is told about an actress called Athene. At any rate, let us keep the story in America. Years ago a play opened in New York and Sir John went to the first night and a supper party afterward. He found himself sitting next to Margalo Gillmore, who was in it, and she asked him how he liked the play. He said, "I liked it very much, except for one dreadful actress called Margalo Gillmore." She replied, "I beg your pardon, I am Margalo Gillmore," and he quickly said, "Oh, I don't mean you, I mean the other Margalo Gillmore."

One time Sir John was directing a production of a Wagnerian opera and von Karajan was conducting. During a dress rehearsal the set was being put up, the stagehands were wandering back and forth, and the costume designer was onstage sticking everybody full of pins. Gielgud was trying to tell his actors what to do but nobody could hear him over the music. Finally, Sir John couldn't stand it any longer and flew down to von Karajan and tapped him on the shoulder and said, "Stop that terrible racket."

☆

Another time, Sir John was rehearsing in Peter Brook's production of *Oedipus*. Mr. Brook could be very artsy-craftsy, and one day he told the cast that they must all make believe they were trees and the next day he told them all to make believe they were deck chairs. Gielgud hated this sort of thing and knew that it had nothing to do with acting.

On the third day Peter Brook told the cast that they should try to frighten him. Some of them screamed at him, and some of them booed and yelled and all kinds of scary things. Gielgud came up to him and said, "We open in ten days."

☆

Backstage before a matinee of *No Man's Land*, I was sitting in his dressing room and I told him about a friend of mine who had been to a Forty-second Street movie theater and overheard somebody say, "You're sorry, you're sorry. You pee on my date and you're sorry?" John said he had one much better than that. In the same kind of movie theater in London he overheard a woman in a very upper-class English accent say, "You terrible man, you've come all over my umbrella."

GILLMORE, MARGALO

Margalo was brought to my flat at the Hotel Elysee by a great friend who has since joined the feathered choir. I asked her if she would like a drink and she said she would like a tiny bit of Scotch. I always take people at their word and I gave her a tiny bit of Scotch, which was gone in a second. She immediately said, "May I have another tiny bit of Scotch?" Many tiny bits of Scotch later . . .

☆

I was dining at the Hotel Algonquin and Margalo was at the next table with another lady and two gentlemen. A waiter came along with two large bowls of soup on a tray, tripped, and spilled the steaming soup on the friend's backless evening gown. She slowly rose in terrible pain, trying to remain calm. As she rose, Miss Gillmore also rose in sympathy and horror. She was about to assist her friend to the ladies' room when some idiot said, "Aren't you Margalo Gillmore?" She was so excited somebody had recognized her that she forgot all about her friend and flew over to the woman and said, "Oh, yes" and started talking about her career in the theater.

GINGOLD, HERMIONE

During the run of *A Little Night Music* in London, Princess Margaret wanted to meet Jean Simmons, so I took the two of them and Jonathan Aitken to supper. Gingold was furious that she wasn't asked, so I made another date to take *her* to supper. The supper party grew to eight people, but being one of the producers I felt that I had to do it. I hired a Daimler and driver for the evening, and after the theater, we went back to the Berkeley for supper. Gingold ordered asparagus, so everybody else did, and it became a very expensive meal, with wine, etc., etc. I kept the car waiting to take her home, and she lived miles away. I took her to the door, where there was a German shepherd that was about to remove my hand. I saw her in and she didn't say thank you or what a lovely time she'd had. However, she did say, "No wonder you like London, ducky, you live in the lap of luxury."

I also took her to tea one day in the garden of No. 10 Downing Street when Harold Wilson was Prime Minister. He made a speech and Gingold in a very loud voice said, "Who writes his material?" People (rather old) kept coming up to her to say nice things about how they remembered her *when,* and she was rude, rude, rude. I told her how rude she was to all these old people who remembered her *when,* and she said, "People who think about the past have no future." Gingold is now close to ninety.

Hermione has always had a string of lovers (all young and rather attractive). Pretty she is not, and her wigs look as if bees would nest there. She is always talking about how common everybody is, while spitting food all over you. I once saw her pass a mirror at a private party, look at herself, straighten her wig, and say, "You're gorgeous."

She had a Yorky years ago that was also very old and became very constipated late in life. When she took it out on the street to do its nonsense, her patience wore out. If the dog couldn't do anything, she would pick it up by the neck and shake it—very hard.

Hermione had two grandchildren living in England whom she had never seen. When she was in London playing in *A Little Night Music* she decided to get a car and driver on her day off and drive out to the country to see them. As she approached the house, which was on a hill, the children came running down the hill shouting, "Granny, Granny." When she saw them coming in hot pursuit she quickly looked at her chauffeur and said, "Driver, drive on."

GISH, DOROTHY AND LILIAN

I had taken the boat from Sorrento to Capri with Dorothy and Lilian and the three of us were sitting together. Suddenly Dorothy grabbed me with great intensity and begged me to go to the other side of the boat. When we got there Dorothy lit a cigarette and inhaled with passion and said, "She won't let me smoke."

GOLDMAN, MILTON

By all rights he should have written this book. Like the good theatrical agent he is, he never stops dropping names and introducing people to each other with full billing and credits. He would get the cream of the theater at his cocktail parties and once introduced me to Lord Olivier at least four times. His finest moment, however, came when he introduced a woman to her husband.

GORDON, MAX

Max was a layman's idea of a typical producer — cigar and all. There was an actress in one of his plays who was an elegant beauty and a friend of mine. He passed her in the hall of the theater one day and said, "You've got a lot of class, let's fuck!"

GRADE, LORD

Somehow, when I see him, the title breaks me up.

GRANT, CARY

What is his secret? Is it gaining weight? Is it no exercise? Is it letting his hair go white? Is it his publicity man? Is it his genes? Is it his attitude? What? What? What? Oh, God! What is it?

HAMMER, ARMAND

Hammer went to Russia as a young man and was told that if he learned one hundred words in Russian he would get along. He had to make a speech to some Russians and when he finished the audience applauded. He was very pleased indeed, turned around to his guide, and said, "Isn't it wonderful, they understood me." His guide replied, "They thought you were speaking English."

HAMMERSTEIN, DOROTHY (MRS. OSCAR)

Dorothy is one of the most wonderful and generous women I have ever known or will know. I used to dine with Oscar and Dorothy at their lovely town house at least once a week. I would go to all of Oscar's first nights, out of town and in town.

One day Oscar was directing one of the 10,000 revivals of *Show Boat* and some idiot was singing "Only Make Believe." He stopped singing, came down to the footlights, and said, "Do you think this song holds up the action?" Oscar said, "Is that your opinion?" And idiot actor said, "Yes." Oscar said, "Oh."

☆

Dorothy told me that when she was on her honeymoon with her first husband she would walk around the ship and Oscar would always be coming in the opposite direction. Every time he passed her he would say, "Hello," and he kept saying, "Hello, hello, hello." Finally, she got bored and went to sit on a deck chair. Oscar came over and sat on the edge of the chair and looked into those wonderful blue eyes and said, "If I were a little boy and you were a little girl I would carry your books home from school." She fell in love with him on the spot, came home from her honeymoon, got a divorce, and married him fifteen minutes later.

HART, KITTY (CARLISLE)

Kitty is very nice and soignée, and I always go swimming with her when she visits Claudette Colbert. We sing musical comedy tunes all the time.

At one point there was some talk about Claudette's doing the London production of the musical *Coco*, which Katharine Hepburn had done in New York, and Kitty was going to coach her vocally. My own opinion (even though I think Claudette would have been better than Miss Hepburn) is that it would have been a little bit like the lame and the halt leading the blind.

HART, MOSS

One of Moss Hart's earliest jobs in the theater was as an office boy with Gilbert Miller, the producer. Mr. Miller had heard about a new door that was sound-proof. He had one installed and asked Moss Hart to stand in his office and shout as loud as he could, anything that came to his mind.

Moss Hart went into Mr. Miller's office, closed the door, and started to yell, "Oh, Mr. Miller— you're hurting me—oh, please stop hitting me—oh, no, how awful—oh, that hurts—" He then opened the door and asked, "Could you hear me?" and Gilbert Miller said, "Every word and you're fired."

HARTFORD, HUNTINGTON

He came up to me at a party looking very pleased with himself and asked me what I thought he had paid for his tie. I told him I thought he had paid one dollar. He looked very sad and said that was what he had paid for it.

HEATH, EDWARD

While swimming in Barbados in front of the Sandy Lane Hotel, he suddenly popped up out of the sea and I asked him whether he was Edward Heath. He said, "Unfortunately, yes."

HELLMAN, LILLIAN

When I was playing in Boston in *Bells Are Ringing* I was not happy with my tiny role. I saw Lenny Bernstein at a party (he was there with the first production of *Candide*). I told him how I felt, and he said to come to the theater (the Colonial) to meet Lillian the next day, which I did. He brought me up to her and he was wonderful about me, telling her how funny I was, and that I had been in all his shows. She looked at me grimly and said, "Can you play forty-five?" (I always used to look young for my age.) I was dying to say, "Can you write comedy?" I have to take the curse off that story and say that I think she was a wonderful writer and a very strong, special lady.

HENIE, SONJA

I met Sonja Henie many years ago in Florida. If you like ice skating she was very interesting.

I tried and tried to get her for the lead in *Harold and Maude*. One doesn't approach Miss Hepburn through an agent or a lawyer (at least I didn't). I have a friend named Ben Strobach who devotes his life to female stars. He approached her for me. She would have none of it. She felt that Ruth Gordon had done it. I didn't want to take no for an answer. I thought she was not the kind of lady to whom one would send an arrangement of flowers, so I found and sent her some lilacs. She called Ben and said that they were the most beautiful lilacs she had ever seen, that the note was perfect (it had taken me sixteen hours to write three lines), and that I should be at her house at 6:15 on Monday. I thought, What do I wear to see her? I arrived at 6:15 in a gray flannel suit and was told to go upstairs. She was seated in something that looked like a very elegant barber chair, didn't say hello, didn't say anything except, "Sit there," motioning to a small chair lower than hers. After about an hour of talking, talking, talking about the theater in general, about Laurence Olivier and how wonderful he could be, and also how less than wonderful, and how great they were together, she looked at me and said, "You're a very persuasive young man. I'll tell you what I am going to do. I'll read the play again and I will call you in the morning. This is ridiculous, but I don't have your phone number. Give me your phone number."

The next morning my phone rang at about 7:00

and that voice said, "Is Frank Milton theayah?" I said, "This is Frank Milton," and that voice said, "This is Katharine Hepburn." I was longing to say, "Who the hell else could it be?" Anyway, she didn't do the play.

HILL, JEROME

I never saw Jerome in an overcoat that wasn't at least thirty years old and he never earned a penny in his life. When he died he left about 30 million dollars. I spent a weekend at his place in Bridgehampton. The house was falling apart like his overcoat, and when I arrived he was in the living room with all the paint falling from the ceiling. I took one look at the mess, thought about the overcoat, and said, "Jerome, your money is old enough—spend some of it."

HILSON, MILDRED

She is a doer of good deeds for hospitals and things, for whatever the reason. When *Equus* opened I had to flee from my flat because I received eighty-seven phone calls an hour. When *Harold and Maude* opened I received one phone call the next day from Mildred (a backer) and she said, "Don't be sad." She also looks smashing for her age—any age.

HITCHCOCK, ALFRED

Crossing on the old *Queen Elizabeth,* I noticed that Hitch was on board. I loved to walk around the deck every day and he used to come at me constantly from the opposite direction. I was convinced that I was in a Hitchcock film.

HOLLIDAY, JUDY

After we opened in New York in *Bells Are Ringing,* the *Wall Street Journal* said that I was a very funny man. We had been running about three weeks and were playing a rather dreary Wednesday matinee. Jerome Robbins had choreographed the bows, starting with the chorus and the minor players (I was one) and leading up to Judy. That day, we all took our bows and then it was Judy's turn. Something overcame me, and as Judy stepped out to take her solo bow, I did, too. The entire cast rocked with laughter. The curtain came down and when Judy passed me in the hall she said, "Don't let the *Wall Street Journal* go to your head, Frank."

I auditioned about fifteen times for that show — sang, danced, read — and then they asked me how well I could play the piano. I wanted to say that I could put a broom up my ass at the same time, but as

I am a gentleman I didn't. I worked so hard for three weeks to get the number at the piano just right and then Jerry Robbins said not to bother, that they would play the music in the pit. The song was still perfect for me even minus the piano. We opened in New Haven, and two critics mentioned me. Judy again passed me in the hall and said, "You sing so well, Frank." The next day the number was out.

HOLMAN, LIBBY

Libby had a nightclub act that I went to see and afterward she came over to the table and asked how she was. I told her that she was terrible and she said, "Thank you." Like most people, she never listened.

HOMOLKA, OSCAR

When I was a child and people asked me where I was the previous night, I thought it was none of their business. I would say that I had been out with Oscar Homolka. Years later I crossed with him on the *Andrea Doria* (not the time it sank) and we played gin rummy all the way home. When I arrived I could finally tell everybody that I really was with Oscar Homolka. The only thing he really liked about America, he said, were the cold cuts.

HORNSTEIN, ROBERT

Bobby's family owned some kind of cat food company. He had a magnificent villa in Capri years ago and was the great celebrity seeker of all time. (Maybe I am calling the kettle black.) I didn't like him and he didn't like me.

One day I was walking up to the piazza from the Quisisano Hotel and I ran smack into Noël Coward. He gave me a big hello and said, "Let's meet in the piazza later and have a drink," which we did.

Noël was not one of the last of the elegant spenders, and I couldn't get the waiter, so I took the bill and went up to the bar to pay for the drinks. Bobby Hornstein came up to me, gasping for breath and shaking all over, and said, "Is that Noël Coward you are sitting with?" I said yes— I had captured the plum. Then he asked me if I would introduce him. I thought to myself that it was a small island and he would meet him anyway, and I told him I would but please, not to make a big fuss.

In a minute he came over to the table and I introduced him to Noël. He pulled up a chair, sat down, and said, "I am giving a big party tomorrow night in your honor. I will have Beatrice Lillie, Lena Horne, the Marquesa this and the Principessa that—" He had about eighty people at the party and I wasn't invited.

INVERCLYDE, JUNE

She lived at the Ritz Tower in New York and had some money. Years ago, she was seeing a director who wanted his own theater in a town house. One day he called her and said that he had found the perfect house with a theater already installed, and she said, "Wonderful. How much are you going to put in?" His answer was, "About seven inches."

IRELAND, JOHN

My first season in summer stock in Martha's Vinyard an old woman was raped and murdered. Everybody in the company and staff was under suspicion. John Ireland was the stage manager, and all the actors and staff lived in a ramshackle house with one bathroom. One night we came back to the house and John came into my room and said he was very nervous and could he move his bed into my room. I was very nervous, too. They hadn't found the murderer yet, so I said of course. When he settled in the room he said that the murderer could come in through the window, so "Let's lock it." He also locked the door. He got into his bed and I got into mine. The moon was shining through the window onto his hands, which were the largest I had ever seen, and I suddenly thought, Oh, my God, he's the murderer. I did nothing but stare at his hands all night.

JEANS, ISOBEL

Isobel Jeans got to be somewhere near ninety, and she was playing in *The Importance of Being Earnest* at the Haymarket in London. Her agent called her about a new play. She didn't want to sign a run-of-the-play contract, so she asked him if there was an out clause. He said, "Out clause? For what, the grave?"

JENKINS, FLORENCE FOSTER

Probably the most untalented woman who ever lived, Florence used to give recitals at Carnegie Hall. She was so awful that the theater was packed. Everybody would stand and cheer when she finished her performance and go backstage to see her and tell her how brilliant she was; and she would believe them.

JONES, T. C.

I played Beverly Carlton in *The Man Who Came to Dinner* in Bucks County and T. C. played Lorraine Sheldon. One night I sat in his dressing room and watched him make up and turn himself into a woman—one of the most macabre things I have ever seen.

Years before that I was in a flop called *If the Shoe Fits*, based on the Cinderella story, and T. C. was the assistant stage manager. He looked like a rather benign miniature Yul Brynner and he kept telling me please to come and see his act, which I finally did. It was at some rather seedy little drag joint. I was sitting at a table having a drink, waiting for him to join me, when suddenly this tall, ravishing woman came over to the table, looking like Louise Brooks in her prime, and sat down — it was T. C.

JULIANA, QUEEN

It was dusk in Porto Ercole and I was on a friend's yacht. We had to dock next to another boat because the port was so crowded. There was just the owner, the captain, and me on the yacht and I have never worked so hard in my life, scrubbing the decks and all sorts of awful things like that. To get out of doing these chores, I suggested that I go look for a decent restaurant, and I went down a very flimsy, wobbly gangplank, then into a coal barge with nothing to hold onto before reaching the pier. There was a yacht next to us of about the same size, and as I was going down the gangplank a very fat Dutch woman was doing the same, and I grabbed her hand to help her. It would have made a better story if we had fallen into the coal, but still, how often does one get a chance to hold hands with royalty?

KAUFMAN, GEORGE S.

Sitting next to me at the ballet (which he hated), Kaufman kept poking me and asking me the name of a see-through screen (the ballet was Swan Lake). I thought he was putting me on, but he kept asking me. Finally I said it was called a scrim and he said, "That's what I'm going to do."

He used to play a lot of bridge and one night he had a partner who didn't have the foggiest idea about the game. At one point in the evening the partner excused himself to go to the loo and Kaufman said, "That'll be the first time he'll know what he's got in his hand."

KENMARE, LADY

Lady Kenmare was a beautiful Australian with a magnificent villa in the South of France. I went to lunch one day at the Maison Blanche in Cap Ferrat. Lady Kenmare arrived with a very old, tired-looking German shepherd. When she went to the loo for two minutes, I was told that the dog was the most vicious in the South of France, but that he was all right if you were near Lady Kenmare. When she came back I brought her a drink; I brought her another drink; I brought her food; I never left her side. She invited me to Kenya after all this Uriah Heeping, thinking I was the most pleasant man she had ever met. She also told me that she kept a lion in her house. As I am terrified of cats, even tiny ones, I never got around to visiting her in Kenya.

KERR, DEBORAH

A young man in California got a job to announce a big opening night in the cinema world. He was told that all he had to do was to announce the stars' cars as they arrived—Cary Grant's car, Lana Turner's car, and so on. The only one he had to be careful of was Deborah Kerr. Came the big opening night and all the lights were flashing. His big moment arrived and he said, "Ladies and gentlemen, Cary Grant's car." Then the next one drove up and he said, "Lana Turner's car." Finally, "Deborah Kerr's car." Then he relaxed and breathed a sigh of relief, and as the next car came up, he said, "And now, ladies and gentlemen, Alfred Hitchcock's cock."

KING, DENNIS

Mr. King was in a play many years ago and the part required him to die during the second act. One day he overheard the director say, "Let's run through the third act." The next morning his agent was on the phone to the director asking whether there was a third act. The director said that there was. The agent wanted to know why Mr. King was not in the third act. The director explained that Mr. King died in the second act. The agent then suggested they bring him back to life.

KITT, EARTHA

There is an apartment in New York that belonged to the Thomas Fortune Ryan family. They sold it to Alice Duer Miller ("The White Cliffs of Dover"), who sold it to Alexander Woollcott, who sold it to Noël Coward, who sold it to his manager, John C. Wilson, who sold it to Saint Subber. Saint Subber had a black friend (Murry Anderson used to call them Topsy and Eva). The Thomas Fortune Ryan family did not like the idea of that combination going up and down in the same lift, so they bought the apartment back for their son Johnny, who six months later fell madly in love with Eartha Kitt.

LAUDER, ESTÉE

Estée had a beauty parlor appointment and arrived one hour early. She was told she would have to wait, but that they would drive her back to her house. She called her house and said to one of the maids, "Tell the chauffeur he don't have to pick me up."

Noël Coward said that Gertrude Lawrence was seven different women under one hat. Her performance in *Lady in the Dark*, which I saw opening night and seventeen times after that, was impossible to describe; watching her magic was like dealing with sand.

She was always mischievous. When she was playing in *Lady in the Dark* she got bored, particularly without Noël around to make her behave. One night she said to the stage manager as she came offstage, "I think I should have some flowers on my desk." Bert Lytell (God! who remembers him?) was right behind her and told the stage manager that she would eat them while he was talking onstage. And she did.

Danny Kaye was in *Lady in the Dark* and all during rehearsals the producers kept wanting to fire him because they didn't think he was any good. His wife, Sylvia Fine, said to wait, that he needed an audience. Opening night in Boston came. During his big moment, when he sang "Tchaikovsky," he stopped the show cold.

Moss Hart, Hazzard Short, and Sam H. Harris were all sitting in the back of the theater and they all said, at the same moment, "Now we really have to fire him," because Gertrude Lawrence had to follow him right away and sing her big number, "Jenny."

She was in a swing. She got off, nodded to Danny Kaye, stepped stage center in the most beautiful Hattie Carnegie mauve suit, and at that moment changed her whole way of doing "Jenny"—a real striptease, with bumps and grinds and all, without taking any clothes off, and she stopped the show colder. I suspect she had been rehearsing quietly. All ended happily.

I went along to see her in London in 1948 in a rather mediocre play by Daphne du Maurier called *September Tide*. I went backstage to say hello, spent ten minutes in her dressing room chatting, and thought it was time to leave. As I got up, she grabbed my hand and said, "Where are you going?" I said that I was on my way to the Savoy Hotel for some supper. She asked me to wait and have supper with her and we sat up talking until 3:00 a.m. When I took her home she said she didn't want to ruin my holiday, but any night I had nothing to do I should please call her because *she* had nothing to do and nowhere to go after the curtain came down.

She loved to misbehave onstage and told me that she couldn't have any fun onstage in *The King and I*. Much later in the run I went to see her again and she was so ill, her stockings hung on her legs, and she had no strength left. She had been ill for a long time and wouldn't tell anybody about it. Finally she died during the run and asked to be buried in her ball costume for *Shall We Dance*. She is buried in Dennis, Mass. Somehow I think she really would have wanted to be buried in England. Her funeral was like an opening night. I got a call from her husband's office saying they had a seat for me. I said they made it sound like a matinee, but they said, given all the requests, it was the only way they could do it. All her leading men were there and all the people that went to first nights. When Oscar Hammerstein read her eulogy he said, "Gertrude couldn't sing very well, she couldn't dance very well, she wasn't a very good actress, but she was a star."

LEE, GYPSY ROSE

Gypsy went to Hollywood one year and they asked her what her measurements were. She said, "Exactly the same as they were three years ago, except that everything is four inches lower."

LEIGHTON, MARGARET

Margaret Leighton was very tall, very thin, very English, and very beautiful. I once saw a taxi run into her on Fifth Avenue. The top part of her looked like Olive Oyl bending forward and she kept saying, "Oh, no, Oh don't, oh, no." The taxi finally stopped, she adjusted her clothes, and walked on.

LEVY, ETHEL

Being married to George M. Cohan was her claim to fame. I met her when she was old, in a musical I was in with her called *If the Shoe Fits*, and every day during rehearsals she would arrive in another outfit. I felt sorry for her and would tell her how nice she looked. I would say things like, "Oh, what a lovely hat," and she would say, "Cary Grant gave it to me." Or I would mention her shoes and she would say, "George Cukor gave them to me." Finally I got bored with the whole thing, but she was so used to the routine that I didn't even have to ask and she would grab her earlobes and say, "Claudette Colbert's mother."

LOGAN, JOSHUA AND NEDDA

Casting for William Inge's play *Picnic*, Josh Logan was looking for an actor to play the very macho lead. Every muscle man in New York was there. All day long he kept saying, "Would you take your shirt off, please?" This went on until about seven in the evening, when he was still saying, "Would you take your shirt off?"

His wife, Nedda, came in and quietly sat down beside him. She waited as long as she could and then very gently tapped him on the shoulder, looked at her watch, and said, "Josh, we are going to be late for dinner." He snapped back at her, "Oh, Nedda, will you keep your shirt on!"

LOWENSTEIN, PRINCE

I had lunch with the Prince in Moustique and he was very pleasant, but the only reason that he is in this book is that he is a prince.

LUNT, ALFRED

I only met him once backstage at a matinee of *Oh Mistress Mine*. He was very tall and I was very mute.

What a perfectionist! When he got his first big break in Booth Tarkington's *Clarence,* and he knew it would make him a star, he spent his last dollar on a beautiful cigarette case from Cartier, which he needed in the play. A friend suggested that the audience wouldn't know the difference if he had a cheaper one and he said, "I would."

Many years later he was directing a television production of *The Magnificent Yankee* and he worked and worked the cast until a few minutes before they were to go on the air. His last-minute injunction to the actors was, "Now I want you to make believe that you have had two martinis."

MANLEY, MARION WARREN

A fat alcoholic of a certain age, who used to make wee wee in the wrong places. I ran into her one day and said I had heard she made wee wee on a banquette of the Ruban Bleu nightclub. She said that was a dirty lie — it was the Kit Kat Club.

MARGARET, H.R.H. THE PRINCESS

I am pleased to say that I know the Princess quite well and have spent a lot of time with her. She has always been wonderful to me. When I produced *A Little Night Music* in London she wanted to see it with me and she also wanted to meet Jean Simmons and have supper with her afterward. I had to get a date for Jean, and as Jonathan Aitken wasn't married then, he was just right.

I really didn't know what to do, so I called H.R.H. and she suggested we go in her car if Jonathan would pick me up first at the Berkeley and then drive to Kensington Palace and leave his car there. She has a delicious red station wagon. It was like the parting of the Red Sea when we arrived at the Adelphi Theatre. I don't think she enjoyed the play very much, but we waited for Jean, who arrived and curtsied right to the ground.

The four of us went to Annabel's for supper, and when we arrived the Princess wanted to go to the loo but didn't want to go without Jean. (Why do women always need company?) Jean shook her head no, but P. M.'s hand motioned rather strongly and it looked like a royal command, so she went. After we were seated for about fifteen minutes, Jean said, "Would you forgive me, Ma'am" and started to leave for the loo and Princess Margaret said, "Of course, you didn't go before."

One night while we were dining in Barbados at the Sugar Cane Club there were twelve for dinner, and I was seated on Princess Margaret's right. Everybody at the table was English except me, and H.R.H. said to me, "Let's rehearse, and when we get back to Maddox (Oliver Messel's house) we can perform." Her memory for all the American show tunes was amazing. She even sang "A Person Could Develop a Cold." The rest of the table started to listen and she asked them not to pay any attention, that we were rehearsing. We started to sing some of the English songs and got to "The Stately Homes of England," which had a very tricky lyric, and suddenly she made a mistake and I forgot and poked her and said, "No, no, darling." There was a deathly hush at the table and I thought for a minute that I was going to be sent to the Tower of London. Then she said, "You really like me." In an instant I said, "Nevertheless, Ma'am." I wasn't about to play *that* game!

☆

Usually she was the easiest guest one could wish for. However, one day I flew to Moustique with Verna Hull to have lunch with her. H.R.H., as usual,

82

seated everybody and put me on her right. During lunch she whispered in my ear that she was coming to stay with us at Verna's house for two weeks.

On the way back, Verna was a nervous wreck. "I am not prepared, I don't have the proper staff, and her bedroom won't be air-conditioned." I told her not to worry, that Princess Margaret would be an easier guest than I was. And she *was*, never complaining about anything, until one day she decided to be difficult.

Verna served lovely cold lunches on the beach in front of her house with all kinds of delicious salads. H.R.H. ate very, very little and one day Verna asked her: "Ma'am, I always give you the same lunch. Wouldn't you like a little something different?" Princess Margaret thought very slowly and said, "I would like a three-and-a-half-minute egg," and Verna asked her if she would like some toast. She quickly said with disgust, "No, no, no, no toast." We sat down to lunch and I was starving and couldn't wait for the three-and-half-minute egg. Verna had two very grumpy maids who had to walk all the way from the kitchen, but at last the egg arrived. P. M. sat up very straight and tapped her egg, took off the top, looked at it, and said, "Egg's not done enough." I saw Verna twitch on the left side of her face, but she couldn't do anything except call the grumpy maid from the kitchen, who walked all the way back to the table, took the not-done-enough egg back to the kitchen and came back again with another egg. P. M. again sat up very straight, tapped the top of the egg, looked at it, and said, "It's still not done enough." Finally the egg again arrived and P. M. said "I'd like some toast." With that I thought Verna was going to fall into the sand. She got up and fled into the house, slammed forty-seven doors, broke three of them, took seventeen tranquilizers, and then arrived back at the table and said, "I'm sorry, Ma'am, but you should have seen me in my drinking days," and H.R.H., who was quietly eating her egg, said, "Oh, but I did. I don't see any difference."

One night her companion Roddy Llewellyn was there and we played a game of categories. I had told Her Royal Highness how pretty she looked (and she did, after she had washed her hair) and she said I should change back into shorts, "You look very good in shorts, so let us be comfy." This was long before the film *Ten* and it was my turn in the box and the category was sex appeal. Roddy said, "Nine," Verna said, "Nine," and P. M. thought for a bit and said, "Seven and a half." Roddy said, "Ma'am, you have to take his age into consideration," and she said, "It was one of the things I did."

The next day she had a struggle getting out of the sea and I went to help her onto the beach and she said, "Nine and a half, and if you remove that hideous thing (I have a bunion) from your foot, I will make it ten."

MARTIN, MARY

I went to the first night of *Leave It to Me*. She became a star in fifteen minutes when she sang "My Heart Belongs to Daddy." Unfortunately, there was a dreadful woman sitting in front of me wearing an enormous hat, which she refused to remove, so I never saw her.

MARX, GROUCHO

Groucho was at a party and there was a terrible little boy kicking the guests and interrupting everybody's conversation. He beckoned the child over and took him upstairs. In about twenty minutes he came downstairs without the child. After some time the boy's mother, somewhat concerned, came over to Groucho and asked him what happened. Groucho said, "He's fine. I just taught him how to play with himself."

MATTHEWS, A. E.

Matthews lived on and on into his nineties. He used to like to take naps in the dark, on his back, on the floor of his dressing room before the play started. A new call boy knocked on his door, which was ajar, saw him lying on the floor, ran down to the stage manager, and said, "Mr. Matthews is dead." Right behind him was Mr. Matthews, who tapped him on the shoulder and said, "Young man, the next time you see me in that position I probably will be dead. However, you say, 'I *think* Mr. Matthews is dead.' "

MAYER, LOUIS B.

Mayer was a very righteous man who had a manicure once a week and always told his secretary not to disturb him while the manicurist was doing his nails. He would sit in a big chair while, as Harold Pinter would say, she would consume his male member. He had a darkened glass ceiling in his office and one day in the throes of ecstasy he looked up to the heavens and spied some workmen, laughing and pointing at what was going on. He immediately looked down at the busy manicurist and said, "You awful creature, what are you doing down there? Get away from there, go away."

MAXWELL, ELSA

While touring in a summer-stock company of Somerset Maugham's *Our Betters*, I became quite friendly with Elsa. I played Freddie, the dancing master, and had to teach her how to do the conga. She wore a red wig and looked just like Fiorello La Guardia in drag. She told me that she knew everybody who was famous all over the world and I said, "What do you mean, *everybody*? Did you know Hitler?" and she said, "Yes, very well." I asked her what he was like and she answered, "My dear, he was a bore."

MENDL, LADY

Thirty-five years ago I had lunch at Elsie's glorious villa in Versailles. I was the first to arrive, followed by Peter of Yugoslavia, Cary Grant, Elsa Maxwell, and several minor celebrities. There were twenty-four guests in all. Elsie was in her nineties and she asked me to play gin rummy with her. I was told by her amanuensis, Hilda West, that she cheated and to let her. She was very tiny and in a wheelchair by then, but she played a brilliant game, smoked one cigarette after the other, and drank two glasses of gin and grapefruit juice, which was the house drink. She also spoke fluent French to about ten French children, whom she had adopted. While we were playing cards I told her that I thought she was fabulous and she said that she would show me why after lunch, which was also fabulous. After we had eaten, she wheeled herself over to me and told me to follow her. We went from room to room until she came to an enormous gym with all kinds of gadgets to swing on and stretch on and where she told me she worked for an hour every day. I have been doing the same exercises every day ever since.

She gave me the worst cold I have ever had in my life, but it was worth it to have dinner with her. She was one of the greats and probably the most relaxed performer who ever lived.

She was in rehearsal for a musical with a score by Vernon Duke. She went to him one day and asked him what a certain lyric meant and he said he didn't know. She said, "If you don't know, how is the audience going to know," and left the show, which turned out to be a flop. Her instincts were perfect; she had very few flops.

Her taste in the theater was just right for what she did, but her taste in her apartment made Mae West's flat look like Elsie Mendl's.

She had nerves of steel, or maybe no nerves. On opening night she passed a young chorus girl who asked her if she was nervous and she said, "Nervous, why should I be nervous? I know all my lines."

I was privileged to see her last performance at Carnegie Hall. What an evening. The audience went mad and she sang and sang, seemingly without strain, at the top of her voice. The audience wouldn't let her stop and finally she just sang with the piano. She sang a song I suspect she had always wanted to sing, "Someone to Watch Over Me." When Gertrude Lawrence sang it to a little doll it was plaintive and wonderful. When Ethel Merman sang it she clearly didn't need anyone to watch over her and it didn't work and she knew it. She took a deep bow and said, "Goodnight, ladies and gentlemen."

MESSEL, OLIVER

I had dinner after dinner at Oliver's house, Maddox, in Barbados. What a gifted man. Not only was there that wonderful show of his work at the Victoria and Albert Museum in London last year, but he was responsible for many houses in Barbados and Moustique, even though you are never quite sure where the bathroom is and whether it will work. He called everybody "darling"—oh, darling, this, and oh, darling, that—and he meant it. I can never understand why he wasn't knighted and neither could he.

All the Messels were very vague, and Oliver's mother was the vaguest of all. Oliver told me that he heard her on the phone one day saying, "Oh, I am so terribly sorry—oh, dear! Oh, that wonderful husband—gone—oh! how awful for her—I must call my vintner and send her some champagne—I feel so awful—oh! yes. What? Oh, oh, I didn't quite catch the name."

In closing about Oliver, I think the greatest compliment paid to him is the number of babies in Barbados named Oliver.

MIEHLE, EILEEN (SUZY)

Suzy has always been very nice about me, and while I had my hot fifteen minutes as a producer, she wrote column after column about me. I don't know how old she is, but she looks eighteen.

MOLYNEUX, CAPTAIN EDWARD

Edward had the most exquisite taste of any man or woman I ever met. I used to dine at his flower farm in Biot in the South of France with this broken-down contessa or that broken-down marquesa, for three or four seasons. Years passed and the poor man started to lose his memory. Vagn Riis Hanson (known as the Great Dane) called me up and asked me to dine at Oliver Messel's house one night in Barbados, because I was the only person on the island who knew Edward. I arrived early and Edward arrived last, was introduced to me, and hadn't the foggiest idea who I was. I let it go and finally we went to table. Halfway through dinner he suddenly said, "My God, it's Oscar."

MONFREDI, CONTESSA

When I dined with the Contessa in her beautiful villa on Capri, next door to the Punta Tragara Hotel, she spoke about the owner of another hotel and she said he was Mafioso. The following night I dined with the owner of the other hotel and he said that the Punta Tragara was Mafioso. For all I know, the whole island is Mafioso.

MONK, JULIUS

Monk was very grand when he used to introduce the acts at Le Ruban Bleu and would always say, "I draw your attention and applause to . . ." whatever the act was. At other times, still being grand, he would say, "Irregardless of what you think."

MONTAND, YVES

I have been told that we look alike, but I like to think that if Yves Montand mated with Beatrice Lillie I would be the result.

MOSES, GRANDMA

Dorothy Gish told me that she was at a dinner party with Grandma Moses and told her that she thought she was amazing for her age and asked how she accounted for her success. She replied that all her life she tried to do her best and if it didn't work out she would say, "Ish Kibbible."

MOSTEL, ZERO

I rode in an elevator with Zero once and he was so proud of the fact that his pants didn't fit, for he had lost sixty pounds quickly. Three weeks later he was dead.

MUNNINGS, LADY

Lady Munnings (wife of Sir Alfred Munnings) had a Pekingese that she adored to such a degree that after it died she had it stuffed and carried it about with her.

While it was still alive but getting very old, it used to make wee wee all the time. One day she was in a taxi and the dog made wee wee all over the seat. As they were getting out the driver muttered, "That's it, no more dogs in the cab." Lady Munnings swept past him and said, very grandly, "I did it!"

NAMARA, MARGUERITE

Marguerite was a very flamboyant Irish woman who wore outsize jewelry and plenty of it and signed everything with a large flourish. She also was a great beauty. She studied singing with Caruso's teacher, and I am happy to say that I studied with her.

She had been married four times, always to very rich men. While I was studying with her, she said, "I pray to God for one more millionaire." At the age of eighty-five she got one—and he kept her, which is more remarkable than marriage at that age. I asked her if she had to do anything (he was 98), and she said, "Oh, no, I just rub his titties every now and then."

NATHAN, GEORGE JEAN

A marvelous critic, who really knew and passionately loved the theater. He was always the first one in his seat on an opening night. He could write with great acidity, though, and he once said that the three most terrible words in the English-speaking theater were "Cornelia Otis Skinner." Actually, she was not a good actress, but she was a very good monologuist (not in a class with Ruth Draper, but who is?) and a charming writer (*Our Hearts Were Young and Gay*).

NEDLANDER, JAMES

Having produced *Otherwise Engaged* with him, I can say that he is a very nice man and a good business partner. I called him up very early on in production and asked him a question about the publicity man and he said, "Frank, I don't know anything about the theater; I know about running theaters."

I never saw him until opening night, when we sat in front of a television set after the final curtain waiting for the reviews. They were raves, and he said, "I think we have a hit." I don't believe he liked the show or really understood it, although of all the plays with which I have been connected, *Otherwise Engaged* was my favorite. Even though *Equus* was a "theatrical triumph" (as Clive Barnes said in *The New York Times*), I think *Otherwise Engaged* is a better play.

☆

It is very difficult to get a quick answer out of Jimmy. He is always pacing up and down or fiddling with papers in his office. One day, sitting opposite him, I simply asked him how he was feeling and between the phone and the pacing and the fiddling I never got an answer. He kept talking about "This here *Annie*," which he had put a huge sum of money into. I don't think he knew what a huge success the show would be.

NIVEN, DAVID

What charm! I met him once at the Connaught Hotel in London and we exchanged some jokes. His were better than mine, but he did write mine down in an elegant little book.

NIXON, RICHARD

We have the same doctor, which is the best I can say for him.

NOLAND, NANCY

Nancy Noland was in that perfectly dreadful review *All in Fun* and was the most eager woman I have ever met. When we went into rehearsal she had about six songs (among them "It's a Big, Wide, Wonderful

World") and was in ten sketches. As we got nearer to the opening, the sketches were changed and the numbers moved around and then her sketches were cut and her numbers were cut until she had nothing left except a deep bow, with a lovely corsage from her boyfriend, on opening night.

NOVELLO, IVOR

The English public adored him. He was one of the handsomest men in England and also one of the nicest. He did a musical every two years, which ran for at least two years.

From the beginning of his career, there was a funny little woman with a funny little hat with a funny little feather. She had no talent, but every two years she would come and audition for him and every time Mr. Novello would say very kindly, "Thank you very much." She kept coming and coming and finally, after about sixteen years, he couldn't stand it anymore. When he saw her standing in the wings, he called the stage manager over and told him to tell the funny little woman that there would be a part for her in the show and that she didn't have to audition. The stage manager went over to her and said that Mr. Novello said that there would be a part for her in the show and that she didn't have to audition and she said, "Oh, dear, but I only do auditions."

NUGENT, ELLIOT

Nugent was a brilliant director and actor, but he had mental problems and had to be confined many times to various institutions. Saint Subber told me that he visited Elliot at the Ritz Tower Hotel, where he had a suite. During one of his lucid periods, when Saint was speaking to him about a new play he wanted him to direct, Elliot was walking around the room discussing the play, being very clear about everything and drinking a cup of tea. He was living on the twenty-sixth floor and as he passed one of the windows he just threw the cup and saucer out and went on walking and talking about the play.

OLIVIER, LAURENCE (LORD OLIVIER)

Olivier is probably one of the greatest English-speaking actors who ever lived. He was playing *Macbeth* in some dreary little town in England, doing a Wednesday matinee, and the audience was awful. Somewhere in the middle of the first act he noticed a nice couple who were staring intently at the stage and he decided that he would play the entire performance to them. In the middle of the second act, he looked out to the audience to see if the couple were enjoying themselves and they had left.

ONASSIS, JACKIE

I met her at the French Embassy and she came backstage during the run of *Otherwise Engaged*. I found her quite tall. She is included here because, given the title of this book, how could she not be?

OUSPENSKAYA, MARIA

One of a group of scene-stealing, head-shaking actresses. The wiggle-waggle went from side to side. One night she went backstage to see John Gielgud and was sitting in his dressing room with her head wiggling away from left to right and he said, "I wasn't very good tonight." She stopped wiggling for a beat, shook her head up and down, and then went right back to the left and right wiggle-waggle.

PARKER, DOROTHY

Never knew her, alas, but I have two favorite stories. She had a rather large drinking problem and decided that she would go to A.A. She went to one meeting and told a friend, "Do you know what they wanted me to do? They wanted me to stop drinking."

When her husband died, the coffin was in the living room of her apartment and a very close friend was there commiserating with her. As they were wheeling the coffin out the door, the friend asked her if there was anything that she could do, and Dorothy Parker said, "Find me a new husband." Her friend said that that was the most callous thing she had ever heard, and Dorothy Parker said, "Oh, then get me a ham on rye."

PETER, KING OF YUGOSLAVIA

I was at a cocktail party in, of all places, Sag Harbor, Long Island, walking around the garden where, as in England, nobody introduced anybody, when suddenly this poor, pathetic creature stood up and said, "King Peter"—not bothering to say, "I am."

PINZA, EZIO

When the opera star opened in *South Pacific* in Boston, an English actress friend of mine was walking through the Commons with Josh Logan, who had directed the musical. He asked her what she thought of Mr. Pinza and she said she thought he was marvelous until he started to sing.

POOL, MARY JANE

The former editor of *House & Garden* is a good friend. She had a maiden aunt in Missouri who used to talk to herself in the mirror. One day her aunt's door was ajar and Mary Jane passed by and heard her aunt say to the mirror, "Louise, you deserve a piece of fudge," which is what I think of when I want to buy myself something I don't need.

PORTER, COLE

I came home from Europe one year and auditioned for *Out of This World*. I had the nerve to sing "Just One of Those Things" for Cole. When I finished he walked down the aisle, with his tiny tie, malacca cane, and boutonniere, and said, "Where did you get your shoes?" I told him Italy and he said that they were the nicest pair of shoes he had ever seen. "You must be in the show," he said. And I was.

PRINCE, HAL

I had a very happy experience with Hal on the production of *A Little Night Music* in New York. By accident I ran into him one evening on Fifty-seventh Street. The next day I was speaking to an old friend of mine, Ben Strobach, who had worked for Hal and he told me he was going to do a musical version of Ingmar Bergman's *Smiles of a Summer Night*. Even though I felt that Bergman was a cinematic giant and that Hal was a very slick Broadway theater man, it all sounded like a wonderful idea. It was very special indeed, and the musical won the Tony and made a very nice profit. There are still dribs and drabs trickling in.

There was some talk about a London production, but it did not materialize right away. I was busy with *Equus* at the time. However, as soon as I was free, I sent a note to Hal and we did *A Little Night Music* in London. We got fabulous reviews and we thought it would be a bigger hit there than in New York, but it wasn't. We ran one year and just about broke even.

When I came back to New York after the opening, Hal called to ask me to come to his office. Steve Sondheim was there and fell all over me, which was not usual. We went to have a drink and Hal pushed his chair back, gulped, and said that he had never offered this to anybody before but that he loved working with me and would I like to be his partner? I said that I was very flattered and would like to think it over. Hal is a very enthusiastic man and I think he was disappointed that I didn't jump at the chance. He said that he would have a copy of Sondheim's new musical, *Pacific Overtures*, sent over to me in the morning.

In those days I was still living at the Hotel Elysee. When the script arrived, I turned my phone off and told the hotel not to call me. I read the book with great care—one does not treat this kind of offer lightly. I got up, had a glass of water, and then read it through again. When I had finished I went to the telephone and called Hal. He asked me what I thought and I said I couldn't sell what I didn't love. Incidentally, I asked, what happened to Pearl Harbor? A history of Japan without Pearl Harbor? Hal said he hadn't thought of that and I said that I did. Then Hal said, "I'll buy that," and thought of who else he could get. The partnership had come to an abrupt end.

PRINTEMPS, YVONNE

When Noël did *Conversation Piece* in London, he sent Romney Brent (who was bilingual) to Paris to work for months with Miss Printemps on her English. He called her to the theater in London the day before rehearsals without the rest of the cast and asked her, "How is zee English?" and she said, "Very gooooood." He thought he had better ask her to go onstage and sing the opening line of the verse of "I'll Follow My Secret Heart," which is "A silver cloud has passed itself across the sky," and she sang, "A sealver clude has pissed itself across the ski." Noël said, "I think we have to go to work."

RAINER, LUISE

I crossed on the *QE II* with Luise and her charming husband and have seen her a few times in New York. She has one major problem—she thinks people recognize her.

REED, JOSEPH VERNON

Reed loved the theater for a while and then realized he couldn't win at it and wrote a book called *The Curtain Falls*.

Leonard Sillman (who produced the *New Faces* revues) had a yellow pad and every day he would look at his list—from Walter Chrysler to Huntington Hartford to Joseph Vernon Reed—of rich, potential backers. Every day he would call them on the phone and ask for money for shows, or for what he called "personal backing." This would go on and on and on. Sometimes Huntington Hartford would come to the phone and sometimes Walter Chrysler would—but never Mr. Reed.

One day Leonard was sitting in his office and the door bell rang. It was Joseph Vernon Reed, who was quickly ushered into Leonard's office, where Leonard immediately conned him out of $10,000. As Reed got up to leave, Leonard's inquisitiveness overcame him and he asked Mr. Reed why after all this time he suddenly just popped in the office and he said, "I had to see the man who called me 147 times without my once calling him back."

REWALD, JOHN

This art historian friend of friends of mine, May and Fran Weitzenhoffer, invited me to stay in his citadel in Menherbes, near Marseilles. How does one turn down an invitation like that one? My mouth was drooling for some Cavaillon melons, and even though he had warned me that he had a very vicious dog staying in his home (I had visions of all kinds of Doberman pinschers or Rhodesian Ridgebacks), I decided that I couldn't say no, even though I am terrified of dogs.

The day I arrived I was a nervous wreck thinking about the dog, and when I stepped into the living room, looked down, and saw the tiniest dachshund I had ever seen, I thought the whole thing was a joke. However, seven minutes later I was bitten in the leg and every seven minutes for the next seven days every part of my anatomy received some kind of puncture. I might add that I have never been back for two reasons—one is obvious and the other is that I have never been asked.

RENAUD, MADELEINE

It was a cold, damp, rainy Sunday in Paris and nothing could be colder or damper or rainier than Paris in midwinter. I got up early, went to a service at Notre Dame—it was beautiful—then went to the Marche aux Puces, saw nothing, and, chilled to the bone, went back to the Relais at the Plaza Athenée for some onion soup, which was bliss.

After lunch, I wanted to go to bed, but I had tickets to see Madeleine Renaud in Jean Louis Barrault's *Harold and Maude*. I went and saw one of the greatest performances I have ever seen in any language. When the curtain came down I sat in my seat sobbing for twenty minutes.

I should have gone to the French government and brought that production to New York, but I thought it would be impossible for an American audience and I thought I could do better. I couldn't and didn't, and that's the end of that boring subject.

RICHARDSON, TONY

While he was directing the film *Tom Jones*, he was having lunch at a rather upper-class house in the country in England and he asked the hostess and all her guests if they would like to come and be extras and they all said that they would adore to. They went on location, and he explained the scene to them: it was a Sunday and the town whore was coming out of church. She had disgraced the whole village and he said that they should ad-lib little English barbs and should say whatever came into their heads. He started shooting the picture, and the town whore (Diane Cilento) came out of the church. Over all the ad-libbing in an upper-class English accent that could be heard from Yorkshire to Timbuctoo, a lady shouted, "Take that, you eighteenth-century cunt."

ROBINSON, BILL (BOJANGLES)

About the only thing really worth watching in the terrible disaster called *All in Fun* was Mr. Robinson. I stood in the wings every night. As we had only three performances, I never got bored.

ROBSON, FLORA (DAME)

I had a friend in London with whom I used to giggle all the time. He was called Bryan Michie. He was 6'6" and played Dame in pantomime. It took him fifteen minutes to get up. In a very confidential mood one night I asked him if he had ever had an affair with a woman and he said, "Yes, Flora Robson once jerked me off."

ROGERS, TOMMY

Tommy had a job with Metro Goldwyn Mayer to take visiting Hollywood movie stars to first nights, because he was very handsome and looked marvelous in dinner clothes, but he had a drinking problem.

I was touring Mexico in 1946 with a group of friends, among them Tommy Rogers, and we stayed overnight in a charming little place called Fortin, where they had gardenias in the swimming pool. We arrived late in the afternoon and I had to share a room with Tommy. I was trying to settle in and unpack and he was on the phone trying to order a drink in English. He looked at me pleadingly and asked me to help him. Very annoyed, I took the phone and shouted at him, "What do you want?" Timidly, he answered, "Scotch, soda, and some ice, please." I then ordered in Spanish and he said he was amazed that I had been in the country for only a few days and I could do that. I retorted rather nastily that any moron could. In a few minutes there was a knock on the door and I went to open it. Standing there was a cheerful Mexican maid with three rolls of toilet paper!

ROMANOFF, PRINCE

At Suzy Gardner's house one night in Southampton, Long Island, I found myself standing next to the Prince. Just to make conversation, I suggested that he go back to Russia and start a counterrevolution, and with great eagerness he asked me whether I thought it would work.

ROSE, BILLY

I am pleased to say he was much shorter than I am. I saw him only once, years ago, when I went to his house to ask his advice about collecting, and he told me I didn't have enough money to collect anything but chess sets — I didn't.

ROSE, DAVID

Noël was playing his nightclub act in Las Vegas and he saw David Rose. He went up to him at the bar and didn't say "How do you do" or "Good evening" or anything. He just started to sing "da, di da, da, da, di da, da" from "The Syncopated Clock"—and it wasn't David Rose.

ROSSE, COUNTESS

The Countess is Tony Snowden's mother and a beauty. I used to see her all the time at her brother Oliver Messel's house in Barbados. To be friendly and aloof at the same time seems difficult, but she achieved it. I suspect the only thing that ruffled her was that her son upstaged her by marrying Princess Margaret.

ST. HELIER, IVY

Ivy played the nurse in Laurence Olivier's *Henry V* and sang "If Love Were All" in Noël's *Bitter Sweet.* She was a lovely minor English actress.

When she got too old to work, an old friend of mine, Murry MacDonald, took care of her. He paid the rent on her flat and all her food bills and took her out to dine once a week. She was very grand and difficult in restaurants. None of this bothered Murry.

The only thing that did bother him was that he could never find out how old she was and neither could anybody else. (She had to be somewhere in her eighties.)

One night, very late, he got a call from the police station. She had been in a motor accident. He dressed quickly and hurried to the police station. As he came in she was lying down, gasping for breath, and he heard the police officer say, "You're Ivy St. Helier," and she sat up very quickly, batted her eyelashes at him, and very coyly said, "Yes." He then said, "How old are you?" to which she fainted away and got back into her lying-down position. The police officer never got an answer, and Murry never found out her age, and as both he and Ivy have both joined the feathered choir, none of us will ever know.

SARAWAK, RANEE OF

The Ranee lived in Barbados for many years and the only thing I can really remember about her is that she was a mass of bunions.

SHAFFER, PETER

When I was trying to raise money for *Equus*, I got a call from a man in the dress business. I could tell over the phone that he was smoking a cigar and the kind of man he was. If I told him it was a play about the loss of the gods of our youth, or if I said anything the least bit intellectual I would lose him. I said it was about a boy who fucks a horse and he immediately, with great excitement, said, "How much are the units?" I said, "$5,000," and he said, "I'll take four."

I told Peter Shaffer, the author, the story later and he said, "That's what the play *is* about."

SCHILDKRAUT, JOSEPH

I did a television show with him on *Omnibus—Every-man* (*Jaederman* in German). From the first day of rehearsal he never spoke to anyone and was immersed in his role of Death. He had nothing to do but call out "Jaederman, Jaederman" (played by Burgess Meredith, who never knew his lines, which was a little nerve-racking for the rest of the cast, as the show was telecast live). We rehearsed from eight in the morning and we went on the air that afternoon. As I passed Joseph Schildkraut's dressing room he was staring in the mirror saying, "Jaederman" over and over.

The broadcast was at four and at the end of the performance Mr. Schildkraut called out, "Jaederman, Jaederman." Cut—over—finished—done with. Then he shook everybody's hand and said hello for the first time.

☆

When he made his debut in Vienna at the State Theater, the part called for him to wear a beard. His father, Rudolph, the great Austrian actor, was in the audience and everybody was watching the father more than the son. He was doing all the things with his beard that an actor should not do: he pulled it, he twirled it, he stroked it. Finally his father couldn't stand it any longer and he stood up in front of the whole audience and shouted at the stage, "Beard, vere are you going vit my son?"

SCOFIELD, PAUL

When he was in New York with *A Man for All Seasons,* I went to a supper party that Scofield attended. There was an English actor there, whom I am pleased to say had a very short career. He had been to the Actors' Studio that afternoon and was imitating all the American actors. He was funny for about five minutes and then my back went up and I said, "The English can do their thing and the Americans can do theirs, and I defy John Gielgud, as great as he is, to play Stanley Kowolski in *Streetcar Named Desire.*" Mr. Scofield motioned me over and we talked about the theater for hours. When it was time to go home we came down to the street and it was pissing with rain. I said, "Why don't you have a car and driver in your contract like most stars do?" He replied, "What would the other players do?" No American actor would be *that* democratic.

SHANNON, HUGH

I knew Hugh when he was playing at the Numero Duo nightclub in Capri and he was married to Betty Dodero, who adored him. He used to drink a lot during his act and sweat a lot and forget his lyrics. Betty would sit next to him and fan him and wipe his brow and give him all the words he forgot.

One night, I went with a few friends, among them Noël Coward, to hear him play. Hugh sweated and drank and forgot and Betty fanned and mopped and whispered the lyrics. Noël was a wonderful audience, and when the act was over he went up to the piano, put his arms around both of them, and said, "It's the best act of its kind I have ever heard."

SHELTON, JIMMY

Jimmy is a very funny man and not ungifted, having written some lovely tunes, among them "A Boy, a Girl, a Lamplight." He told me that his mother went to Lily Daché's and bought a one-of-a-kind hat for $125. She went to a large cocktail party the next week and at the other end of the room there was a woman with the same hat. For a moment she was livid and then she thought, Oh, what the hell, and motioned to the woman, pointed to her own hat, and made funny faces and gestures. The woman looked aghast and turned away. Jimmy's mother thought, Silly woman, no sense of humor. When she got home and looked in the mirror, she saw she was wearing a different hat!

The other hat story Jimmy told me was about a woman who had bought an expensive Easter hat with lots of flowers on it. She was wearing it on the way to a cocktail party, but first she had to go to a funeral. As she came into church, she realized that the hat was too frivolous and she handed it to one of the ushers to hold for her until after the service. She was about to sit down in the church when she saw the usher coming down the aisle with her flowered hat. He kept walking past her and placed it on top of the coffin. After the service, the coffin came up the aisle with her hat on it and she thought, I've got to get my hat back. So, even though she wasn't at all close to the family, she went out to the grave. As they were lowering the coffin into the ground with her hat on it and the preacher was saying, "Ashes to ashes," she started to cry and the family was very touched, not realizing that she was crying for her hat.

SHERWOOD, ROBERT E.

Sherwood was at a cocktail party when there was a sudden silence and across the room one could hear in a very loud voice, "By the way, whatever happened to that dreadful faggot, Robert E. Sherwood?" All 6'6" of Mr. Sherwood reached over to the little man who made the remark and said, "I beg your pardon, but I'm Robert E. Sherwood," and the little man

112

looked up at him and said, "You are? Well, whatever happened to you?"

SHEVELOVE, BURT

Burt, who directed *A Funny Thing Happened on the Way to the Forum,* was invited to George Cukor's lovely house in California for dinner one evening, and being a dandy, he spent the entire day planning and primping. He arrived at Mr. Cukor's house completely overdressed. He rang the front door bell and Cukor himself answered the door dressed in torn sneakers, jeans, and an old sweater. Cukor took one look at Burt and said, "At our age, it's enough to be clean."

Burt had rented Oliver Messel's house in Pelham Place and one freezing day he was sitting in front of one of those tiny English heaters with a blanket on his feet and one on his shoulders, shivering. The maid came in and said, "Oh, sir, it's colder outside," and Burt answered, "It's supposed to be."

He had another maid in England—real Cockney—and one day while he was watching television she was standing watching it, too, with a cigarette dangling out of her mouth. They were showing some

113

old newsreel shots of Hitler, who was yelling and screaming and waving his arms and jumping up and down, and the Cockney maid said, "Oh, that 'itler, 'e's such a fidget."

SILLMAN, LEONARD

I was in three of Leonard's shows: *If the Shoe Fits*—one month; *Happy as Larry*—three performances; *All in Fun*—three performances. So I knew him quite well.

One of Leonard's backers was a rich man in the electronics business by the name of Julian Sprague. Leonard borrowed $10,000 from him and said that he would return it as soon as his mother's estate was settled (it was probably worth about six drachmas). Mr. Sprague said okay and never said a word about it for years. One day he was talking to Leonard over the phone about backing for *New Faces* and he asked him if his mother's estate had been settled and Leonard forgot for a minute and said that it had been settled for months. Julian said, "Leonard, you are a liar and a cheat, and unless I get my $10,000 within the week my lawyer will call your lawyer." Somehow Leonard scraped up the money and paid off the debt. About ten days later Julian Sprague suddenly died and Leonard called a friend and said, "That idiot, why couldn't he have died two weeks ago?"

☆

All in Fun was my first Broadway show, and even though it ran only three performances in New York, the stories are endless. There was a singer in the cast by the name of Dorothy Dennis, who later became the wife of Alfred Strelsin. I suspect that he invested a few dollars in the show for her sake and she was given a very brief song to sing downstage left, with no light on her, and a headdress by Irene Sharaff that would have hidden Kate Smith. She sang:

> *I want to do the macumba*
> *The way they do in Brazil*
> *I'm growing weary of rumba*
> *Of tangos I've had my thrill.*

She then would go offstage into the wings. While she was singing the brief song the set was being changed. I played a Swami fortune-teller and mimed a short macumba step while reading Imogene Coca's palm. The entire chorus was onstage doing the macumba, and at the back of the stage was an enormous drum with a great Brazilian discovery (never heard of since) on the drum, singing at the top of his lungs — *Macumba*. Night after night out of town, Dorothy would sing her four lines, but one night she came off and said, "I think they are fucking me up onstage." I asked her why she thought so and she said, "I think something is going on behind me."

We had a dress rehearsal that lasted for about three days — Leonard would take nothing out — and we had our opening night in New Haven at the Shubert Theatre, which had very little depth backstage. There was a young man in the show who was very handsome but with no talent. I think he also had a friend who put some money in the show so he could be in it.

There was a song in the show called "That Man in the White House," sung by Walter Cassell and a very strong male chorus: "That man in the White House/ He'll win the election./ Ump pa pa, ump pa pa, ump pa pa." Crouching in the wings were four young men holding a platform with the very handsome young man on it, made up as Teddy Roosevelt. We were all huddled in a corner and I was the only one who could see what was going on onstage and they kept saying to me, "Now? Now?" and I kept saying, "No, no, not yet." Onstage, Walter Cassell was still singing with the chorus. Suddenly I looked out and the curtain had come down. We never got on and the audience never knew who that man in the White House was, which was just as well because by then it was about 1:30 a.m.

SMITH, KATE

Tallulah Bankhead was on Kate Smith's radio show and while they were on the air Kate Smith said to her to count to three after she walks onstage. Tallulah's reply was, "Are you going to tell me how to make an entrance, you big fat tub of shit?"

STEARNS, ROGER

Roger had a lovely restaurant on East Fifty-fourth Street, backed by friends, among them Cole Porter. I used to dine there all the time and Roger was a good friend and a gent, but he was a very nervous host. While he would play his very nervous piano, he would be watching everything going on in his restaurant.

One night an Irish drunk came up to him and said, "Play 'When Irish Eyes Are Smiling' " and Roger played. When he finished, the drunk again said, "Play 'When Irish Eyes Are Smiling' " and Roger played, and when he finished the drunk started to cry and fled from the restaurant. I went up to Roger and asked him why he hadn't played, "When Irish Eyes Are Smiling" and he said that he had and I told him that he had been playing "My Wild Irish Rose."

STREISAND, BARBRA

I first saw her in a terrible musical called *I Can Get It for You Wholesale,* and when she finished her first song I ran up the aisle and called an agent friend of mine and said that I had just seen an enormous star. The agent asked her name. I told her and she said, "I know her — she's so ugly she'll never get anywhere."

STOTESBURY, MRS. EDWARD

She had a lovely house in Palm Beach, and one day when she was taking some friends on a tour she came to the dining room and said, "All my silver is gold."

TALMADGE, CONSTANCE

I can't drink very much and never could, but years ago I used to get pissed with Constance every night. The next morning she would call me on the phone, suffering as much as I was, and say, "Let's meet at the Monkey Bar of the Elysee, but no drinking."

We would meet at five and Constance would rationalize like all drunks, "The doctors all say one drink is good for you. Waiter, may I have a Scotch and soda, please?" That was gulped down in one second. Then she would say, "You know, there's grain in it. Waiter, may I have another Scotch and soda, please?" This would go on and on until we both got pissed all over again.

Old, old men used to come up to her all the time and say that they remembered her in this film or that film. She looked marvelous for her age and for the amount of booze she consumed, but she always insisted that she had been a movie star when she was sixteen years old.

TANGUAY, EVA

Eva lived to be a very old woman and she was famous for one song, "I Don't Care." About one year before she died she got a booking at the Palace Theatre when it was strictly a vaudeville theater. She had the most important spot in vaudeville—next to closing.

This ancient woman would arrive very early and creep onto the stage and stay in the wings bent over almost on her hands and knees listening to the orchestra and watching all the acts. She would start to jiggle about with her arms and legs and she would get jazzier and jazzier and taller and taller, and when it was her moment to go onstage she was a young woman and would run on the stage and bounce up and down and sing, "I don't care, I don't care." The audience would cheer and she would go back into the wings and sink into being an old woman again and slink home into the night—back on all fours again.

TAYLOR, ELIZABETH

She was always backstage when Richard Burton was playing in *Equus* and kept telling me how tired she was while he was onstage killing himself.

Burt Shevelove told me he went to a dinner party that she was at in Venice. He had never met her and he was thrilled to be sitting on her right. For quite a while she kept talking to the person on her left. Finally she turned to him and her first words were, "I haven't had a good shit in three days." Mind you, that is *his* story!

TAYLOR, LAURETTE

The good Lord has been very kind to me in many ways, and one of them was that I saw Miss Taylor in *The Glass Menagerie*—one of the truly great performances.

A very important actress went backstage to see her and flung herself at her feet, begging for her secret. Miss Taylor, who was a very shy person, pulled back, thought for a minute, and said, "I thought Amanda would wear a ribbon in her hair."

TAYLOR, ROBERT

If my life had been different and I had the money that everybody thought I had, I would have moved to Rome. However, I did live there for six months while they were making the film *Quo Vadis* and got a call from the Cinecitta Studios to see the casting director. He asked me if I could ride a horse, and I said yes. He then asked me if I could ride a horse bareback and then jump into the sea. That was the closest I ever came to Robert Taylor.

TODD, MICHAEL

The first night of a play called *Kind Sir*, starring Mary Martin and Charles Boyer, was a stellar event. The play itself eventually was made into a good film with Cary Grant and Ingrid Bergman. During intermission I saw Michael Todd, whom I knew slightly, and asked him if he was enjoying himself. As he shook his head up and down, smiling, he whispered between his teeth, "I'm terrible."

TREVOR, CLAIRE

While I am writing this, Claire is right down the hall at the Scallinatella Hotel in Capri. We were in Kenya together last winter and on the way in our own bus to William Holden's Mount Kenya Safari Club she told me a story about John Wayne.

Everybody told her not to fall in love with him before she met him, but she swore that he was not her type. The first day of shooting, though, she took one look at him and did fall in love, in a nice way. They were on location, shooting a Western, and the whole cast took all their meals together outdoors. George Sanders was in the film and he spoke to nobody. One of the actors tried to bring George Sanders into the conversation. This was long before the word "gay" was used as it is today, and the actor said that in America they had many derogatory words for a homosexual — fairy, sissy, pansy — and was there anything comparable in England? George Sanders thought for a minute, put his knife and fork down slowly, and said, "Yankees." John Wayne leaped across the table, and it took about fourteen men to keep him from killing Mr. Sanders.

☆

Claire was married to Milton Brew, who started life as an agent, hated it, went on to other things, and, I understand, made a lot of money. He bought himself and Claire a beautiful eighty-foot yacht and was very proud of it. There were three in crew and it was all very fancy. They invited Ernst Lubitsch, the great Hungarian director, on the yacht and he arrived with lots of luggage and a proper blazer and all the paraphernalia that David Niven might have worn in a movie about a yacht. Claire's husband welcomed him aboard and the yacht started steaming out of the harbor. They were out about fifteen minutes when Lubitsch said, "Ven do ve get to the yacht?"

TUNE, TOMMY

During the previews of *My One and Only* I went to supper with Tommy Tune, Twiggy, and an old friend, Tommy's agent, Eric Sheppard. The show was in terrible trouble. During supper Tommy and Twiggy couldn't and wouldn't take their hands off each other. It was obvious that they adored each other and I said that if they could get across to the audience what they were doing in the restaurant, the show would be a big hit. They did, and the show was a smash.

TWIGGY

When she was a model and weighed about two pounds, Twiggy went to a dinner party and Princess Margaret was seated opposite her. She was a very young Cockney girl and was in awe of H.R.H., who never said a word to her all through dinner. Finally she looked across the table and said to Twiggy, "You must have another name. What is it?" Twiggy told her what it was and P. M. said, "How unfortunate."

VAN RENSSELAER, PHILLIP

I think it is obvious that he comes from a good family with a name like that. However, I was standing next to him at the Parke-Bernet Galleries during an auction when he said he had to leave and would I bid on a certain chair for him—and pay for it. He left—and so did I.

VEIDT, LILY

Lily was a Hungarian agent married to the actor Conrad Veidt. She never read the newspapers, and her assistants had to tell her who had died every morning. One day one of them came into her office to tell her that George Sanders had died. She was inconsolable and couldn't stop crying. Then she pulled herself together and said, "Take him off the Rolodex."

WALKER, MAYOR JIMMY

When I was a child he used to come to our house. I was about a year old when I felt that he was somebody not quite to be trusted.

WALLACH, ELI

Some people in the theater refer to him and his wife, Anne Jackson, as "The Blunts," which I think is rather mean.

WEBB, CLIFTON

Clifton adored his mother, Mabel. At one point in his life they were both in the chorus together. She lived to be a very old lady, and when she died Clifton was disconsolate. He wept, sobbed, and carried on as though he was the first person ever to lose his mother. He was also very stingy. Noël was a good friend, but not a patient one. Once when Clifton went to pieces during a telephone call, Noël finally had had enough. Remembering how stingy Clifton was, he said loudly and clearly, "Clifton, unless you pull yourself together at once I am reversing the charges." He did.

WEISSBURGER, ARNOLD

Arnold was a very nice fellow—and a well-known theatrical lawyer—who always wore a flower in his button hole. He also adored his mother, who went on and on, and everywhere that Arnold went, his mother was sure to go. Every year he used to take a suite at the Savoy in London for himself and his mother and give large cocktail parties. One night she said good-bye to Mae West and Arnold said, "Mother, that was Rebecca."

I have been told that one day he got a call from a newspaper saying that they wanted to do an article on typical people who were staying at the Savoy having breakfast. Arnold rushed out to buy himself a new dressing gown and a peignoir for his mother. The next morning breakfast arrived with a lovely white tablecloth and a rose and a reporter from the London *Daily Mirror*. Both mother and son were photographed and interviewed, but when the article appeared in the paper a few days later, it was completely derogatory and was intended to show, in a left-wing newspaper, the ghastly people who stayed at the Savoy.

WEST, MAE

I got a call to audition for Miss West and had to go over to Broadway after her show to meet her. I waited backstage for one hour after the curtain came down. At last she came out of her dressing room, and about eight chairs were lined up on stage, so that everybody's back was to the audience. Out she came. She never stopped moving and humming, even when she was sitting down. Finally, I came out and she hummed and said, "You look sexy to me. Now let's see what you can do. What about some taps." I told her that my tap dancing was almost nil, but attempted a few steps. When I finished, she said, "Mmm, you still look sexy, but you can't dance."

WINDSOR, THE DUCHESS OF

Somebody wanted to write a book about her called *Untitled*. What a pity they wouldn't let him.

WHITEHEAD, ROBERT

In 1947, Noël hired me to be a standby in *Tonight at 8:30* for seventeen parts. We did six plays—the original production was nine. I got a call from Robert Whitehead after we had been in rehearsal for a week to offer me a part in *Crime and Punishment*, starring John Gielgud as Roskolnikov. He said it wasn't a very big part but that it was very effective. I had one big scene onstage alone with Mr. Gielgud (he had not been knighted as yet), where I had a great telling-off speech.

I told Mr. Whitehead that I was sorry but Noël had hired me and I felt that I couldn't leave. He said that I was a fool, that *Tonight at 8:30* was going on tour and that I was only the understudy, and that *Crime and Punishment* was opening in New York and would be much more important for my career. I still said no.

We had what was called a pre-Christmas lay-off in those days, and I went to the first night of *Crime and Punishment.* Toward the end of the first act the stage cleared of people except for John Gielgud and a funny little Russian man, who looked at Raskolnikov and said "Murdered" and the curtain came down. That was the part.

WILLING, DONALD NEVILLE

As far as I know, Donald is still wobbling about in London. During World War II he ran a thing called Bundles for Britain, a worthy cause. He stayed in America for many years and finally decided to return home to England. One rare, bright Sunday morning he was in the country and he was thirsty. He was lunching in a small restaurant and asked the waitress if he could have some ice water. She rather brusquely said, "I beg your pardon?" and he repeated that he would like some ice water. She left and sent over the owner, a hockey-stick lady who rudely asked him what he wanted. Once more he pleaded for some ice water. She fled in horror and a few minutes later she came back with one piece of ice in her hand, then threw it into his glass saying, "I've just taken it off the fish."

WHITTY, DAME MAY

She was a very old lady when she played in Emlyn Williams's *Night Must Fall,* and she broke wind constantly. Also because of her age, she was terribly deaf, so always thought she was sneaking them out. One night she was onstage at the opening of the second act and was playing Patience while Mr. Williams sat at her feet. The opening line of the dialogue was "Danny, Danny, it won't come out." One second after she said it, she let out a real rouser and Williams had to run into the wings.

ZADORA, PIA

An awful actress, I thought, who finally got a job playing the young girl in *The Diary of Anne Frank.* Her performance was so terrible and the audience hated her so much, that when the Nazis came for her at the end of the play, the audience shouted at the stage in unison, "She's in the attic."